# For the Souls of Black Folks

# For the Souls of Black Folks

*Reimagining Black Preaching for Twenty-First-Century Liberation*

Cari Jackson

CK *Publications* · Eugene, Oregon

FOR THE SOULS OF BLACK FOLKS
Reimagining Black Preaching for Twenty-First-Century Liberation

Pickwick Publications
An Imprint of Wipf and Stock Publishers
199 W. 8th Ave., Suite 3
Eugene, OR 97401

www.wipfandstock.com

ISBN 13: 978-1-62032-300-7

*Cataloguing-in-Publication data:*

Jackson, Cari, 1956–

 For the souls of black folks : reimagining black preaching for twenty-first-century liberation / Cari Jackson.

 xxvi + 172 pp. ; 23 cm. Includes bibliographical references.

 ISBN 13: 978-1-62032-300-7

 1. African American preaching. 2. African Americans—Religion. I. Title.

BV4208.U6 J33 2013

To my Mom and Dad, Gladys and Robert Jackson, *in memoriam*, whose love for God and commitment to church ministry have shaped me and continue to inspire me.

nd to all those who have been wounded by their experiences in church.

# Contents

# Acknowledgments

THIS PROJECT BEGAN YEARS ago when I was a little girl growing up in
nd so, there are many people who have participated in some
way in bringing this to fruition. I thank each one of you who challenged
and prodded me in your own way.

There are numerous colleagues, friends, family, and congregants—
who have encouraged me and prayed for me throughout this process.
Thanks to all those who lovingly accepted limited time with me as part of
their support for this project. Special thanks go to my mentors Dr. James
. Forbes, and Rev. Frederick E. Dennard for the rich conversations we
have had through the years about preaching ministry. Special thanks to
my doctoral advisor Dr. Traci C. West for helping me to clarify the focus
of my project and to stay on course. Thanks to the congregations I have
journeyed with over the years that have taught me much about the kind
of pastoral leadership needed today—Church of St. Paul and St. Andrew
nited Methodist), First Presbyterian Church of Brooklyn, The Riverside
Church, and First Congregational Church of Stamford.

Thanks and love to my family, especially Sheila Outing, Robin L. Ow-
ev. Dwight Jackson, Jenny Vallon, Rev. Candy Holmes, Rev. Karen
inda Randall, and Rudy Jackson who provided me the emotional
support I needed to get through this project with a measure of sanity and joy.

# Introduction

Like other churches our church has veered off on every conceivable side path, which interferes with and nullifies its chief duty of character building. It has built up a body of dogma and fairy tale, fantastic fables of sin and salvation, impossible creeds and impossible demands for unquestioning belief and obedience.[1]

WHILE CHASTISING THE CONGREGATION for not living righteously enough, the tall black preacherman wearing his papal-style mitre,[2] long black robe, and stern face, bellowed, "For some of you, I am the only God you will ever see." This claim was made in the 1960s by my first childhood pastor in an all-black Pentecostal church of almost 1,000 members. In response to his proclamation, some congregants privately expressed their confusion and disapproval, but no one publicly questioned the statement nor challenged the preacher who made it. Instead, the only public response from the congregation was, "Amen. Amen."

Not long after this proclamation, the preacher took a course of action that resulted in a major schism in the church. The schism was not in response to this declaration of his demi-god status, but to his secret

Du Bois, *Crisis Writings*, 330. Taken from in a speech he delivered at Fisk Univer-
Also according to Diane Judith Nash, "Charismatic leadership, as we have known it, has not freed black people, and it never will. Because, instead of being a vehicle to liberation, it really is a symptom of social illness. For an adult to think that he or she needs a leader—somebody to tell them what to do and all they have to do is do it—is a symptom of a social illness." "Freedom Riders Documentary," Public Broadcasting. Nash served as a key leader in the earliest days of the Civil Rights movement activities in desegregating lunch counters. She was one of the founders of the Student Non-Violence Coordinating Committee, coordinator of the Freedom Rides aimed at desegregating public transportation, and organizer for voter registration of blacks.

The headdress of a bishop or abbot, consisting of a tall pointed cleft cap.

remarriage. My pastor, although a divorced man himself, had preached adamantly against divorce and remarriage for decades. After divorcing his first wife, he had received a revelation from God that divorce was against the "perfect will" of God, but acceptable by grace as long as one did not remarry. His theological and moral explanations about marriage and all aspects of life went unquestioned and unchallenged. Even as suspicions were widespread that he was engaging in "consensual" sexual relations with several adult females in the congregation, these suspicions were overlooked and excused given that he could not remarry. When he announced to the congregation that he had remarried, hundreds of people left the church, scores of others experienced major health problems (some resulting in death), and countless others who wrestled with significant faith crises left the church and never returned to any church.

Many of these Christians, deeply committed to God, had relied on the word of the preacher to determine not only what was pleasing to God but also what was morally right. What he preached was the definitive word by which the congregation lived their lives. When he, their demi-god, violated what he had instructed them, the theological chaos, the moral confusion, and ethical conflict within the congregation were over whelming. Having relied on the preacher as their moral compass, many were unclear about what was right and wrong, and had little capacity for how to navigate their moral waters.

It was here in my first church that I began witnessing a series of inci dents in black churches —both directly and indirectly—that pressed me to explore the ethical issues of how the power of the pulpit shapes the social agency and moral authority of black churchgoers. Experiences from my own life as well as stories that have received public attention in the media reflect a tradition in black denominational churches for black male (and to a growing extent black female) preachers "to say and do what they wish while preaching" without fear of censorship[3] and to expect the acquies cence and silence of congregations.

## The Personality and Role of Black Preachers

The title of this book, *For the Souls of Black Folks*, is so titled in honor of the seminal sociological study done by W. E. B. Du Bois of black people in the

---

3. LaRue, *Heart of Black Preaching*, 12.

In the course of his study of the lives of black Americans in the late 19th century, Du Bois became the first social theorist to study the development, characteristics, and implications of black churches and black preaching.

Based on interviews with former slaves, his participant-observer research, and review of voluminous public records, Du Bois identifies the three primary features that characterized black Christianity during slavery mancipation as "the Preacher, the Music, and the Frenzy."[5] "The Preacher," Du Bois states, "is the most unique personality *developed by the* merican soil. A leader, a politician, an orator, a 'boss,' an intriguer, and idealist."[6]

For Du Bois, the role of black churches and clergy is to enhance the lives of blacks by 1) teaching morals, 2) inspiring the high ideals of Christ- 3) serving as agents of social and moral reform.[7] Chapter 2, "The Nexus of Racism and Power," examines this preacher personality and preacher roles as characterized by Du Bois more than a century ago, and discusses the question, "What should both the personality and role of black preachers be in the 21st century?"

My first childhood pastor greatly exhibited his preacher personality as "a boss," whose preached words and lived behaviors were to be unchallenged. The result of this was the disempowerment of many in the congregation that left them bereft of a clear sense of their own social agency and moral authority. *Social agency* is the cognitive and emotional ability of individuals to make independent ethical, moral, and political choices and actions as members of a group or society. "Moral authority" is the innate rights, privileges, and responsibilities that individuals have, divinely conferred, to exercise their social agency.

In response to my observations of my first pastor and fellow congregants and countless others since then, I have been troubled throughout much of my life by the normative unexamined social control that black preachers exercise over black churchgoers. What I have observed emerging on the landscape of churches in historically black denominations[8] in recent

While Du Bois' work listed "folk" in the singular, I have decided to use the plural form "folks" to honor the diversities among U.S. blacks. Du Bois, "The Souls of Black *Writings*.

Du Bois, "Souls of Black Folk," 494.

mphasis added.

Du Bois, "College-Bred Negroes" in *Writings*, 837–78.

The use of the term "black churches" used throughout this text refers solely churches within historically black denominations, especially black Methodist, Baptist,

years leaves me even more alarmed about the ways that preacher power, personality, and role are manifest today. What I observe is that preacher power, having gone unchecked and unchallenged for generations, has run amuck. Unchecked, unchallenged, and unbridled, preacher power has a deleterious, even infantilizing, effect on the moral development of both black churchgoers and black preachers.

Because black churches continue to be a major influence on the overall black culture in the U.S., the personality of the black pulpit is, in ways, a det riment even to blacks who are not churchgoers. To say this is not to ignore the ways in which the power of the black pulpit has been uplifting, cathartic, and transformative for untold numbers of blacks. Rather, it is an invitation, even an urging, that black denominational leaders, black preachers, and black churchgoers also acknowledge, what psychologist Carl Jung calls the "shadow side." It is also an urging to be honest about the impact of anti-black racism upon U.S. black church culture in shaping double-consciousness, what W. E. B. Du Bois argues reflects a "twoness—an American, a Negro; two souls, two thoughts, two unreconciled strivings; two warring ideals in one dark body."[9] Unacknowledged, this twoness in the collective psyche in the black church culture contributes to a black preaching tradition that is both liberative and constrictive for the social agency and moral authority of blacks. Acknowledged, the healing needed for the souls of black folks in historically black churches and communities can begin in earnest.

By highlighting the kinds of problems in black communities today, it is my hope that black church can become even more effective in the minis try to which we have been called.

Why is acknowledgement of the two warring souls critical now? To day, there are a few key social factors that make this era greatly distinctive from the late 19th century and early 20th century contexts in which Du

---

and Pentecostal denominations that were formed by African Americans and primarily for African Americans. While I acknowledge that some of the power dynamics explored here may also be found present within certain denominations that are historically white, such as, Assemblies of God and Southern Baptist, the focus here is on the nexus of power and racism.

9. Du Bois, "Souls of Black Folk," 364. Compare with Hogan's typology which distin guishes two types of beliefs: "self-conscious" and "motivational." "Self-conscious beliefs are those that individuals consciously choose regarding particular issues; these beliefs," Hogan asserts, are those which individuals hold and can "readily admit and articulate." Motivational beliefs, however, are those beliefs "that actually guide thought and action." At times, motivational beliefs can contradict, and compromise the self-consciously held beliefs. Hogan, *Culture of Conformism*, 62.

Bois initially explored the personality and role of black preachers. These social factors include: (1) advances in information and communication technologies that are barraging blacks (churchgoers and non-churchgoers) with images of opulent wealth—from commercials, "reality" television shows, television and internet shopping, and more; (2) blacks have enjoyed unprecedented participation in the sports, entertainment and media industries in the past 30 years that lend the *appearance* of major socio-economic advances for all blacks—that is, that blacks "have arrived"; (3) a tremendously widening economic class divide among blacks—mirroring what is reflected in the broader society; and (4) national politics and culture that reflect a mounting disregard, and at times contempt, for working class and mericans of all races.

These factors within the broader culture have greatly contributed to an inordinate emphasis in black churches on wealth attainment, commonly known as "prosperity gospel." The emphasis on financial prosperity and attention to social status can be seen in a "size-of-ministry-competitiveness" that is commonplace. While this competition is often regarded as friendly, some black male preachers have been known to ensure that the seating capacity in newly constructed church buildings exceeds that of preacher colleagues. In the context of these contemporary social factors, the role of preachers, as understood by Du Bois "to enhance the lives of blacks by 1) teaching morals, 2) inspiring the high ideals of Christianity, and 3) serving as agents of social and moral reform" has been relegated to a lesser priority. There are very substantive costs emerging from this shift in priority.

Stories abound in churches across historically black Baptist, Methodist, and Pentecostal denominations where pastors have embezzled and misappropriated funds from churches, engaged in inappropriate sexual relationships—with opposite and same gender churchmembers (youth and adults), and have ignored it when congregational leaders have foregone their a fiduciary responsibilities on behalf of the church in order to gift their pastors with luxury items. There is also a growing phenomenon of foreclosures on church properties as increasing numbers of churches, focused on size as a sign of successful ministry, have built larger edifices which they have not had the resources to maintain, especially in this time of a national financial downturn.[10] These stories whether involving

"In many cases, churches ran into trouble after borrowing to build bigger houses of worship needed to accommodate growing congregations in once-booming housing markets. Shelly Banjo, "Churches Find the End is Nigh," *Wall Street Journal*, January lso according to Pastor Christopher Chappell, Pastor of Grace Community

sexual, financial, or other forms of egregious and unethical behavior by pastors, all share one critical factor in common: the acquiescence, silence, or complicity of black congregants.

A principal example of congregational acquiescence, silence and complicity is observable in the case of Rev. Henry Lyons, former president of the National Baptist Convention. In 1997, the walls of deception concealing Lyons' clergy misconduct began to burn down before his local church congregation, the National Baptist Convention, and the general public when his then wife, Deborah Lyons, was arrested on charges of burglary and arson. The house Deborah Lyons set afire was a $ home that her husband co-owned with his secret lover, a National Baptist Convention (NBC) employee.[11]

In the weeks following the house fire, Lyons repeatedly denied any financial misdoings and his sexual affair. Relying solely on his statements of innocence, the NBC board gave Lyons a unanimous vote of confidence and did not launch any internal investigation. In the subsequent months, numerous records revealed Lyons' use of church funds for the purchase of personal luxury items, oversight of church financial accounts that yielded many irregularities, violation of federal lobbying laws, defrauding lenders of $3-4 million by getting loan and investments funds based on grossly inflated membership numbers,[13] and hiding $4.8 million in a secret bank account with no records regarding the inflow or outflow of the funds.

Even after Lyons' indictment on federal racketeering and grand theft charges, many NBC clergy were still taking "a wait-and-see" approach regarding Lyons' culpability. Once Lyons was convicted for fraud and embezzlement, for almost two years of his sentence in a federal prison, he officially remained the senior pastor of Bethel Metropolitan Baptist Church. The decision to maintain the position open was influenced by

---

Christian Church, "some churches have gotten into trouble by trying to grow too quickly." "11 Alive News," Atlanta NBC-WXIA, February 3, 2011.

11. Jaudon, "Lyons Chronology," *The Tampa Tribune*. The property records of the house listed Lyons as a single man. Prior to the public revelation of the affair, Bernice Edwards already had been convicted for embezzlement. Emerging from this case, she was convicted and sentenced to prison for tax evasion. Edwards died in prison in 2003.

12. Jaudon, "Lyons Chronology."

13. Lyons had claimed 8.5 million members and 33,000 churches. More accurate estimates suggest 1–3 million members and 8–10,000 churches.

14. "Baptist Leader Henry Lyons Faces Charges of Racketeering and Theft," March 16, 1998.

appeals sent by Lyons from jail requesting to keep his position.[15] Although the congregation did finally vote to terminate Lyons as their senior pastor while he was still in prison, they wrestled whether or not to reinstate him upon his release. While the Bethel congregation voted not to have Lyons return as their pastor, within three months of his release from prison, he was called to serve as pastor of another black Baptist congregation. Despite embezzlement, adulterous affairs, and repeated deceptions, church leaders who served closest to him continued to yield to Lyons' authority and the congregants continued to trust him.

The sense of freedom for black preachers to say and do what they choose flows from a tremendous authority and high trust that black congregations tend to bestow automatically and lavishly upon their preachers. Shaped by this church culture, it is common for black preachers to expect to be regarded as the boss, whose God-given authority is never questioned. As one preacher claims, "I am the pastor, and I am *supposed to be* in charge."[16]

While this approach to preacher power is a cultural norm within historically black churches, little attention has been given to the ethical responsibility present in the pastor-congregation relationship and to the implications upon the ethical formation of black Christians. Such a lack of attention to the ways preacher power impacts upon black churchgoers is Lyons' appeals to be maintained and later reinstated as pastor.

yons incident and others like it urge us to reflect on what messages are being taught to black churchgoers—especially children and youth—about the role, responsibility, and power of pastors, and about the relative power and authority of churchgoers. As ethicist Richard M. Gula states,

> t the center of this [pastoral] responsibility is the prudential handling of the inequality of power [between pastor and congregants] When we lose sight of the power gap between us and those seeking our pastoral services, we pave the way for exploiting them.[17]

Incidents like Henry Lyons require black churches and denominations, committed to the holistic liberation of blacks (churchgoers and non-churchgoers) to take a critical look at the messages about preacher power

yons' Trial: The Aftermath," *St. Petersburg Times*, 2006.

This statement was made by Dr. I. V. Hilliard founder and pastor of New Light Christian Center in Houston. Founded in 1984 with 23 members, and New Light Christian Center now has 28,000 members. "New Light Christian Center" television broadcast, aired on the Word Network, May 20, 2008.

*Ethics in Pastoral Ministry*, 75.

that contribute to shaping a culture of congregational acquiescence, silence, and complicity. If black churchgoers are disempowered from developing and using their social agency and moral authority within black church, then how are they to strengthen and exercise this agency and authority to navigate through the power relations and moral issues present in broader culture? Moreover, how are they to develop the tools to participate in the socio-political liberation of all blacks and other marginalized people?

As I look at the relationships that are commonplace between black preachers and congregations, it appears that the "unique personality" of black preachers identified by Du Bois continues to be the prominent personality that directs and shapes black churches. But is this the preacher personality that is most needed in this era? If Du Bois' contention that one of the roles of black preachers is to serve as agents of social and moral reform is still ap plicable today, black preachers must operate with more integrity than seen in some situations today, like that of Henry Lyons or Bishop Eddie

Eddie Long, organizer of a 25,000-person march in 2004 riage equality and avid opponent of gay rights, was sued in young men from his congregation, New Birth Missionary Baptist, alleging sexual coercion. Like Lyons, Long vociferously denied the allegations as each man came forward, and pronounced that he would fight these un truths. As the months proceeded and more information was released about the gifts and promises from Long to these young churchmembers, the four cases were settled out of court in 2011.

Long is one of the three black preachers whose sermons are analyzed in later chapters here to discuss how sermons convey messages about social power. I included Long in this study well before the lawsuits were filed against him. Because of his approach to power as identified here, however, I was not surprised when I learned of the allegations of sexual coercion. While many black Christians have focused on the fact that the lawsuits were filed by men, suggesting that Long's anti-gay rhetoric might have been indicative of a mask for his own inner struggle and perhaps even self-loathing, the critical issues relating to power should not be eclipsed. Long's situation reflects a complex ity of issues that warrant exploration—issues relating to the authority and trust bestowed upon preachers as well as the coercive and secretive culture present in many black churches. Coercion and secrecy extend not to homo sexuality, but a broad range of other issues in black churches.

This investigation of black preaching emerges not only from de cades of my personal experiences with and observations of pyramidal clergy-congregant relationships within black denominational churches, but also from my deep concern about problematic social trends[18] in the lives of the black masses the United States today—namely, disproportionate rates of poverty,[19] high school dropout patterns,[20] high rates of arrest and incarceration,[21] disproportionate health problems,[22] and so on. As the economic gap has widened, masses of U.S. blacks are living in deeper levels of poverty and experiencing a range of other social ills concomitant with poverty. Despite these mounting social problems affecting black masses, the growing trend in black churches is an emphasis on individual prosperity and economic advancement[23] with minimal attention and nominal head-nodding to efforts for social reform.

ccording to a 2011 poll conducted by the Barna Group,

The significance of statistics about such issues as high school dropout rates, college enrolment relative to prison incarceration, health problems (including HIV/AIDS), and poverty are captured in varying ways depending upon the goals to emphasize the overall advancements of blacks or to reflect the social problematics within black communities.

2000, almost one in four blacks (24%) lived in poverty, including 3.5 million %) of black. Blacks are three time more likely to live in poverty than whites. "The merican Community—Blacks: 2004," *American Community Survey Reports*, 1.

2004, the national statistics for high school graduation was 68 percent, reflecting a national dropout rate of 32 percent. The dropout rate for black girls was percent, and for black boys 57.2 percent. Urban Institute, "How Minority Youth Are eft Behind by the Graduation Rate Crisis."

For example, "there were 4,618 black male sentenced prisoners per 100,000 black United States, compared to 1,747 Hispanic male sentenced prisoners per ispanic males and 773 white male sentenced prisoners per 100,000 white males." "Prison Statistics," *Bureau of Justice Statistics*. Also, according to the National nited Fund (NBUF), data from police agencies across the U.S., blacks represented percent of arrests in 1999, although 12 percent of the nation's population. If this trend continues, under current voter eligibility guidelines, more than 30–40 percent of black men will permanently lose the right to vote. NBUF also reports that black students in public schools are more likely to be suspended. See "The Justice System," *Nation Black*

For example, "The share of African Americans without health insurance in 2010 percent and 11.7 percent of whites without health insurance at the same time." Note that the statistics for uninsured Latinos is even higher at 30.7 percent. Nadra Kareem ow the Recession Has Hit Blacks and Latinos." Also, "America's black and Hispanic communities have been disproportionately affected by HIV and AIDS During 2006, % of all new HIV diagnoses and 49% of new AIDS diagnoses were in black people." IDS Statistics by Race," *AVERTing HIV and AIDS.*

See Mitchem, *Name It and Claim It*. Also see McMickle, *Where Have All the Prophets Gone?*

> Churches are not thought of as contributing to civic enhancement, beyond poverty assistance. Most people do not connect the role of faith communities to civic affairs, particularly local efforts like as sisting city government, serving public education, doing commu nity clean-up, or engaging in foster care and adoption, and so on. There are opportunities for faith leaders to provide more intentional, tangible, and much-needed efforts to assist local government, par ticularly as many services have been diminished by the economy.

It is often argued that racist systems and structures of the larger soci ety, as controlled by the white hegemony, are the cause of the deteriorating state of "black America." While much of the declines in black college enroll ment, increases in black incarceration and so on are directly linked to the continued anti-black racism in the U.S., to lay all responsibility on whites for the perpetuation of these social ills lacks intellectual and spiritual honesty. Clearly, if all blame were to be laid at the feet of the white hegemony would that suggest that blacks have no social agency and thus bear no responsibility for our own lives? Does that suggest that anti-black racism has supported the growing numbers of black millionaires and billionaires in the not the agency, acumen, and talents of those individuals that account, at least in some measure, for their financial success? Of course not.

To ignore what we as black Christians—individually and collectively— contribute to our own life circumstances—for good or for ill—cannot with stand honest scrutiny. Why, then, should we continue to ignore the complicity of black churches and black preachers to the social ills plaguing black com munities today? We must ask what socioethical factors contribute to masses of blacks falling through the proverbial "cracks" in this land of opportunity into poverty, under-education, under-employment, over-incarceration, and more.[25] Especially in light of indignities like that of Henry Lyons, and others, it is imperative that black Christians take a more critical look at the ways that the black preaching tradition is not only a major resource for the social and moral direction of the black communities, but has also been complicit in the disempowerment of blacks thus contributing to staggering social and moral ills among blacks.

---

24. Barna Group, "Do Churches Contribute to Their Communities?"

25. Noting the widening economic gap, Lincoln and Mamiya contend that one of the major issues for many black denominations in the 21st century will be "whether black clergy and their churches will attempt to transcend class boundaries and reach out to the poor." Lincoln, *Black Church in the African American Experience*, 384.

For black preachers to function more fully in the role of facilitating social and moral reform that Du Bois speaks of requires a significant, long-overdue transformation of black preaching and worship. Black preachers are challenged to recognize and replace messages that promote the demigod status of black preachers, promulgate a pyramidal power dynamic between preacher and congregation, and impede the full social agency of black worshipers. In place of the commonplace messages that perpetuate preacher-congregant hierarchies, black preachers are challenged to use the dynamic and charismatic style of black preaching to bring forth new messages that facilitate the ethical empowerment of black churchgoers that is sorely needed for the 21st century.

While I recognize that androcentric patriarchy[26] continues to be a mainstay in the black preaching tradition, the examination I offer here extends beyond patriarchy to all forms of oppressive hierarchy often normative within black churches. I do so because ultimately it matters little whether the preacher-congregation relationship is headed by a male or female preacher. The effects of the power dynamics of social control over black worshipers (both female and male) are still the same.

This examination necessarily includes a look at the ways in which congregants in black churches are often socialized to ensure the acquiescence and silence of fellow congregants in order to maintain the pastor's position at the top of the social power heap. And so I ask: (1) What are the impacts of unchallenged acceptance by black congregants of the various proclamations made and spiritual instructions given by preachers upon black churchgoers' own social agency? (2) What are the ethical and moral implications for black preachers who have "unchallengeable" authority? (3) What is black preaching really teaching about social power?

## An Interdisciplinary Approach

This book seeks to address two formidable challenges for Christian social ethics: one, expanding the dialogue within ethics to look more critically at racism, as the canvass upon which a particular socio-historical context is drawn, and its impact upon the ways in which social agency and moral authority are understood; and, two, engaging in an ethics conversation with

---

This challenge expands upon that forwarded by Katie Cannon to confront "inherited traditions for their collusion with androcentric patriarchy." Cannon, *Katie's Canon*, 23.

homiletics and other disciplines to ascertain the influence of preaching on the hermeneutics, understandings, and exercise of social power.

To address these challenges, this study engages a diverse range of sources from Christian ethics, black religious studies, homiletics, sociology, and psychology to investigate the implications of the nexus of the anti-black racial oppression present in the U.S. society and the messages about social power conveyed through the contemporary black preaching tradition. This nexus, I argue, instructs black Christians regarding what the socially accept able parameters are for them as operate both as members of black denomina tional churches and as social agents in the broader society. This nexus shapes the contours and textures of the social control of black churchgoers.

W. E. B. Du Bois' theory of double-consciousness[27] is especially use ful in the quest for a more comprehensive understanding of how racist contexts shape understandings of personal agency. As Du Bois contends there is a bifurcated impact of racism on individual self-consciousness. This theory of bifurcation provides an important foundational method for a text analysis of selected sermons of three contemporary black preachers as il lustrative of the kinds of messages about social power and moral authority commonly conveyed through the black preaching tradition.

Acknowledging the prominent positions that black Baptist, Method ist, and Pentecostal religious movements have held in shaping black Chris tian life and culture in the U.S.,[28] primary attention is given to sermons preached by clergy from these three religious groups—namely, Bishop T. D. Jakes,[29] Bishop Vashti Murphy McKenzie[30], and Bishop E These preachers have been selected because of their respective reputa tions as key actors on the national religious stage, within their denomina tional groups, and beyond. Also, they have been selected because of their

27. Du Bois, "Souls of Black Folk," 365ff.

28. According to Lincoln and Mamiya, almost 70 percent of black Christians are Baptist or Pentecostal (Baptist, 47 percent, and Pentecostal, 22 percent). *Church in the African American Experience*, 136.

29. Jakes was named "America's New Preacher" by *Time* Magazine in pastor of a formerly Pentecostal, now interdenominational church in Dallas, Texas of 30,000 members.

30. McKenzie listed in *Ebony* magazine's "Honor Roll of Great A Preachers in 1997," as the presiding prelate of the 13th Episcopal District of the Methodist Episcopal Church.

31. Long provides "Sexual Reorientation" conferences to help convert homosexuals into heterosexuals, and he is senior pastor of New Birth Missionary Baptist Church, a 25,000-member church in Lithonia, Georgia.

respective influence on other black preachers, and thus, on the landscape of black churches. Furthermore, these preachers are representative of three distinctive paradigmatic preaching approaches to the role of black sermons in the re/production of power relations.

For each preacher, my analyses of ten of their sermons are presented in the chapters that follow. These particular sermons were selected among those that: (1) were identified and marketed by the preachers as some of their premiere sermons, (2) spanned across the preaching years during which the preachers were most well-known, and (3) were preached to diverse audiences, where possible.

While each of these three preachers has roots in a particular religious tradition –Pentecostal, Methodist, and Baptist, it is not my suggestion that the content of their preaching is representative of the denominational group of their respective backgrounds. This is not a study of the actual *effects* on black churchgoers' sense of social agency. Rather, this is a study of sermon texts that explore the themes about social power found in certain models of black preaching and the ethical *implications* of those themes.

To offer a comprehensive analysis of social power relations that have shaped and been shaped by black preaching, this investigation seeks to: ) assess the analytic methods conventionally used to examine the influence of black preaching, (2) develop a more integrated analytic strategy for sermon analysis, and (3) present an analysis of selected sermons utilizing the analytic strategy offered here. Further, this study provides an ethical framework by which to assess the implications of those messages. This ethical framework can later be used to engage in a comparative analysis across other religious contexts.

This study challenges conventional analytic approaches to black preaching by attending to the understandings of social power and moral authority, which are too often unaddressed in the literature on black preaching. This study also presents a theoethical framework useful for examining constructions and dynamics of various social relations expressed in specific contexts. Finally, by providing a distinctive method for contextualizing constructions of social power, this research offers an interdisciplinary analytical approach to investigate how racism has shaped the prescriptions from black pulpits about what constitutes faithful and empowered ways of living for black Christians.

By incorporating a critical normative theory, this investigation of black preaching provides what Iris Marion Young refers to as "a mode of discourse which projects normative possibilities unrealized but felt in a particular given social reality."[32] That is, a critical examination of the values and traditions commonly promoted through black sermons serves as a pathway to new emancipatory possibilities for the influence of black preaching in the lives of black churchgoers.

My goal is to contribute to the critical liberationist discourse needed not only to identify traditions and norms within black preaching that are *constrictive* to the full social agency of black Christians, but also to develop a *liberative* ethical response as to how those traditions and norms can be transformed to contribute more fully to a greater social empowerment of black people needed in the 21st century. By liberative I mean any resource or tool that fosters the development and expression of individual and collective social agency and moral authority to be used in ways that help transform marginalizing and inequitable social conditions, systems, and structures into those that value the dignity and worth of all human beings.

Liberation is often conflated and confused with the economic or social advancement of individuals. While such advancement can and must be fostered in the lives of individual blacks, liberation, however, is not only an individualized experience. True liberation can only be realized in the collective experiences of human beings as they relate to one another within their groups and societies. "Constrictive" is anything—structures, teachings, values, practices, traditions— that impedes the potential of liberation from being realized.

To reflect the generational implications of the black preaching tradition, this study looks at preaching specifically in historically black denominations. This focus is not intended to suggest that the issues of social power relations examined here are not present in churches that are not a part of the historically black denominations. The implications for how sermons in those church contexts shape understandings of social power remain open for a subsequent investigation by others.

While I recognize that issues related to gender are integral to any discussion of power in black churches, this investigation is not intended to be a womanist critique[33] of black preaching. Given the multivalent issues

32. Young, *Justice and the Politics of Difference*, 6.

33. Womanist theology reconsiders the traditions, practices, interpretations of biblical scripture, and theological perspective with a special lens to empower and liberate women of the African diaspora, especially in the U.S. Womanist theology interrogates the social construction of black womanhood in order to offer a liberatory perspective for the black community that factors in the lived experiences of black women. See, for

present in the nexus of race and power mediated through black preaching, what is referred to by Christian ethicist Monica Coleman as "the trajectory of womanist religious scholarship"[34] alone cannot provide the resources needed for a comprehensive critical analysis and ethical reformulation of the influence of black preaching.

This analysis is presented as an experiment in developing a critical race liberationist ethic for preaching intended to utilize and move beyond the bounds of gender-focused analyses. As such an experiment, this analysis engages some of the preeminent scholars in womanist critical theory, atie G. Cannon, Deloris Williams, and Marcia Riggs, as well as the feminist critical lens of such theorists as Iris Marion Young. Further, to forward a critical race liberationist ethic that may have applicability for .S. black experience and other contexts, this study engages liberationist scholarship of such thinkers as Paulo Freire to help expand the conversation of liberationist ethics across racial and religious groups.

In presenting a critical examination of the role of black sermons in the re/production of power relations, I acknowledge the sensitivities that may be stirred in readers regarding this material. Claire Renzetti argues that research is likely to be "sensitive" when exploring issues that impact upon "some deeply personal experience," concerns matters of "social control," or addresses "things sacred to those being studied."[35] This research touches upon all of these sensitive areas. As such, an admixture of emotional and religious issues held sacrosanct may surface for me as a researcher and child of the church as well as for other blacks who have had deep and meaningful experiences in the black church as a collective. And at the heart of this study is a critique of matters of social control within the black church.

enzetti notes that ambiguities of language and concepts tend to be heightened when dealing with sensitive research. With that understanding, I have sought to be clear in my definitions and always to be straightforward and loving in my presentations.

It is vital that black preachers, historically black denominations, and scholars and students of homiletics engage in intentional reimagining and reinventing of black preaching to make it more relevant for the demands of

---

example, Williams, *Sisters in the Wilderness*; and Cannon, *Katie's Canon*.

    Coleman, "Roundtable Discussion: Must I Be a Womanist?," Respondents: Katie Arisika Razak, Irene Monroe, Debra Mubashir Majeed, Lee Miena Skye, Stephanie Y. Mitchem, Traci C. West.

    enzetti, *Researching Sensitive Topics*, 3.

the today's socio-political complexities. The people in the pews and those in the streets need us to reform our preaching with a greater focus on em powerment than on prosperity.

# PART I

# The Holy Trinity of Clergy Power
*Authority, Charisma, and Trust*

The black and massive form of the preacher swayed and quivered as the words crowded to his lips and flew at us in singular eloquence. The people moaned and fluttered, and then the gaunt-cheeked brown woman beside me suddenly leaped straight into the air and shrieked . . ., while round about came wail and groan and outcry, and a scene of human passion such as I had never conceived.[1]

THE MERE WORDS, "I am the chaplain," were often enough for them to grant their trust to me during my hospital chaplaincy training. In situation after situation throughout my chaplaincy training, I experienced incredible authority and trust thrust upon me—even though I was a stranger—by anxious patients, grieving loved ones, and weary medical staff. They did not understand that I was a seminary student in training. I did not wear a clergy collar, only a hospital staff badge displaying my job title "chaplain." Their trust in me, moreover in my role, helped them get through their life challenges and make major life decisions with a modicum of grace and strength.

In addition to trust, there were two other critical elements present in these interactions that enabled me to provide chaplaincy care: authority and charisma. The staff badge that I wore indicated that I had been conferred by the hospital the authority to come into the rooms of these strangers, and into

Du Bois, "Souls of Black Folk" in *Writings*, 493–94.

3

their very personal and intimate space. Once I established the contacts with these individuals, the third element of charisma determined the quality of these connections. My disarming smile and gentle-yet-firm way of relating enabled them to relax, open up, and share whatever they needed to unburden. The unique combinations of the trinity of authority, charisma, and trust gave power a particular expression and influence in these specific contexts.

Being able to trust in another human being, or in a person's role, is critical to the effective functioning of groups and societies. Being able to rely upon the authority indicated by a person's position or role helps lower the anxieties people often feel in stressful situations. The charisma of those who provide services and supports impacts how safe and secure people feel in their life circumstances. But how do we determine where the line should be drawn regarding how much trust we extend, and to whom?
know the authority conferred to someone appropriately reflects their abilities? How do we know when charisma warrants the trust we give?
we understand what power really is?

## Defining Power

Social theorists across disciplines generally regard the "ability to" accomplish a desired goal as a key element of power. Sociologist Max Weber defines power as "the chance . . . to realize [one's] own will in a communal action even against the resistance of others who are participating in the action."[2] Ethicist Thomas Wartenburg presents two distinctive concepts of power—power-*to* and power-*over*—that further help explicate the power dynamics in clergy-congregants relationships. Building upon Weber's definition of power, Wartenburg posits that "power-to" is the ability to accomplish something as intended, whereas, "power-over" is the ability to accomplish something using social control or command over others.

Power-*to* reflects social relationships based in a greater likelihood for mutuality than generally present in power-*over* in that it includes not only the ability to affect someone or something, but also the ability to be affected by someone or something. Power-*over* focuses primarily on "the ability of one person [or group] to control the actions and beliefs of another" and to affect others without them having the ability to reciprocate. Power-over reflects the uni-directional control and influence characteristically present

2. Weber, *From Max Weber*, 180.
3. Wartenburg, *Forms of Power*, 18.

in the dynamic in clergy-congregant relationships. Power-to can be understood as critical for human survival; whereas power-over, as a strategy "to realize one's own will even against resistance."[4]

ere is an example of how power works through its interlocking elements of authority, charisma and trust and how it can be used to help people "accept" the minister's direction. One of my childhood pastors used his power to accomplish his will (or God's will) with regard to the purchase of real property. While the congregation had raised capital funds for a particular property that the congregation had voted to invest in, the preacher, used the power of his authority in the pulpit to inspire the congregation to endorse and adopt his new vision. The power of the preacher's charisma continued over the years even when this new plan did not materialize as

Amidst this unrealized project, the preacher used his power again, to redirect the church trustees and congregation to yet another real estate venture. Despite the sense of betrayal felt by some trustees and others in the congregation, sermons were used again to urge and inspire the congregation to embrace the minister's new vision of a worship center and Christian school.[5] After more than 25 years of neither the school nor the worship center being fully materialized, some of the original congregants who supported the vision have left the church, or died, many others have remained despite the repeated, costly changes in vision.

In this case, and many like it, authority, charisma, and trust working in tandem created an expectation with the preacher and congregation that his direction and vision should always prevail, despite the financial, psychological, spiritual, and other costs to the congregants. Because authority, charisma, and trust are interwoven in the fabric of ministerial power and the clergy-congregant relationship, each of these elements warrants a closer look.

## Authority by Apostolic Succession

In order for power to be present, at a minimum, there must be a sense of authority operating in an interaction. While the terms *authority* and *agency*

Sociologist Martha Long Ice, in a study of how clergy engage in ministry, defines power as that which gets people to "do what you tell them to do;" and authority as that which helps people "understand and choose to accept your direction." Ice, *Clergy World-* lso see her study of women clergy in ibid., 137.

perating a Christian day school had not been discussed within the congregation as part of the church's vision at any time prior to this new vision; it was, however, in this author's opinion that the minister had a personal vision to have a school in his name.

are often used interchangeably, there is a critical distinction between these two. *Authority* is a "right" conferred or agreed upon—explicitly or implicitly—in a specific social relation for one individual or group to engage in particular activities, in particular ways, with particular people, at particular times. Unlike *authority* that refers to rights only acquirable and recognizable through relationships with others, *agency* is an ability innate to all human beings to make personal choices and actions independent of others. This innate ability is not relational or dependent upon what others confer, agree to, or accept. Agency can only be engaged as authority when it is recognized and yielded to by others, and as such, is able to function as power.

In many churches, black and other, it is largely presumed that the authority that ministers have always takes precedent over the human agency that congregants may have. This authority does not have to be earned by ministers, but is bestowed automatically when ministers assume explicit positions and assignments. Ordination, or even self-proclamation as "called by God," brings a presumption of ministerial rights and skills. presumption that accompanies ministerial authority is a presumptive to make decisions for the community, even against the desires, will or resistance of the community. Often all that is needed to exercise this authority is to frame the visions and decisions as "the will of God"—God on whose behalf and with whose permission the preacher is regarded as speaking.

Yet, it is generally unclear how to determine what the minister's will is and what is God's. This lack of clarity stems from the doctrine of *ostolic succession*, which contends that the full authority of God, through Jesus Christ, has been bestowed upon the preacher. Emerging from apostolic succession is the belief that to obey or to disobey the direction of the preacher is tantamount to obeying or disobeying God. As a result, apostolic succession gives considerable power to ministers.

Although the doctrine of apostolic succession runs throughout the Christian tradition, it is strongly present in historically black churches in ways that are unique to black church because of racism. The formation of the black church during U.S. slavery and post-Emancipation mirrors some of key the challenges faced by the early 1st century Christian church as each of these formative churches developed in contexts of close scrutiny, discrimination, and oppression by the political and economic hegemony of their respective contexts. Following the pattern of the first-century church for withstanding oppression, the role of church leadership in the black slave/post-emancipation churches was to foster unity and strength for their fledgling church groups.

In these early fledgling church communities, pastor-centered leadership was deemed essential to the survival of these communities to remain faithful to the correct teachings of Jesus. In the second century CE, Bishop Irenaeus promoted "apostolic succession"[6] as the spiritually-conferred process by which authority was handed down through the church hierarchy, and the only guarantee that church communities would receive authentic

postolic succession was deemed to be the only legitimate process by which both the power and the authority of Jesus passed down to spiritual leaders in local churches.[7]

arly church scholar Hans von Campenhausen contends that it was common to make spiritual endowment from God a precondition of religious authority or regard appointment to office as the evidence of that en-

With this endowment, Campenhausen alleges, there was a goal to foster spiritual *freedom* for all individuals within various church groups,

*equality*.[9] Those who had been endowed with religious authority were understood as having higher status as the leaders in the communities. This endowment through apostolic succession, thus, helped give rise to ecclesiastical authority and hierarchy as interwoven concepts.

ccording to Campenhausen, "hereditary dimension" or "spiritual pedigree," was a critical aspect of how authority was manifest in the early church. The concepts of spiritual heredity and pedigree were designed to "protect the rights of the appointed elders against a rebellious congregation."[10] That is, once elders were appointed as the spiritual leaders of a particular community of Christian believers, they were regarded as having inherited the full of authority of Jesus Christ to lead and teach the people. With the certification as spiritual inheritors of Jesus' authority, privileges and charismata were also conferred upon church leaders.[11] Regarded as following in the spiritual lineage of Jesus, spiritual leaders—bishops, elders, and deacons—were not merely viewed as providing *guidance* to the community, but were to be *obeyed* by the community. As ecclesiastical roles

*Adv. Haereses*, 3.3.1–3.

Campenhausen, *Ecclesiastical Authority and Spiritual Power*, 2.

13.

86.

87.

and offices were formalized, the early church established canon law that approached ministerial authority as an immutable quality by which elders and bishops were to direct order within church communities. Furthermore, canon law established that the relative rights and duties of individuals with in superior and subordinate positions were to be maintained at all times.

Early Christians were instructed how to relate with those in authority— such as, "Do not disregard them, for they are persons who hold a place of honor among you, together with the prophets and teachers." because church unity was essential to early church Christian church survival and identity, disobedience or challenge of spiritual leaders was regarded as disruptive to that unity, and therefore, sinful.[14] Once clergy were appointed by the ecclesiastical heads, the congregations were obliged to follow the cler gy's leadership and could not even consider requesting the removal of clergy for any reason. This approach is strongly present in black churches today.

Black homiletic scholar Cleophus LaRue agrees that black congrega tions continue to bestow a great deal of "authority" upon their preachers. He argues that this authority is not conferred automatically "but must be earned by the preacher through earnest and effective preaching as well as through meaningful association with the 'folks' over a period of time." What LaRue describes is how the stage is set within black churches for cler gy-congregant relationships that are framed by a pyramidal, power-over paradigm greatly fostered by an emphasis on charismatic black preaching.

Also comparable to the early Christian church in which unity was es sential to community survival from social oppression, a sense of unity in black churches has been critical to surviving racial oppression in the The tradition of obedience was further reinforced by the context of slav ery from which obedience to slave masters was transferred to black male preachers and became part of the cultural norms of black churches.

Consistent with the concepts of apostolic succession and spiritual pedi gree, LaRue contends that black congregations typically view preachers as "special representatives of God, or, even more, as manifestations of the divine presence and thus worthy of great reverence and admiration." the teachings and visions presented by black preachers are generally to be re garded as directions from God, and as such, are to be followed faithfully and

---

12. Ibid., 89.

13. Slee, *Church in Antioch in the First Century CE*, 106, citing *Didache*

14. Campenhausen, *Ecclesiastical Authority*, 52.

15. LaRue, *Heart of Black Preaching*, 12.

without question. As was the case in the early church, there is a traditional expectation in black denominational churches that pastors are to be obeyed, and not questioned or challenged.

## Charisma as a Seal of Approval

Perhaps even more strongly valued than ecclesiastically-conveyed authority in black churches is charisma. Sociologists C. Eric Lincoln and Lawrence Mamiya observe, "Black churches place a premium on the charisma of the pastor, a most important expression of which is preaching ability."[16]

This second element of clergy power, *charisma*, is uniquely linked to the personal characteristics of an individual. When charisma expresses itself through an individual's personality or special abilities, it influences others to bestow authority and trust that might not otherwise be given or to greatly expand upon authority and trust already given.

elating to Weber's definition of power, charisma plays a major role in facilitating the realization of a preacher's own will against the resistance of others, using coercive tactics in ways that appear non-coercive.[17] That is, through charming personality and charismatic preaching, black preachers have historically redirected the will of the congregation to be in line with and support the preachers' will. An example of this is reflected in the earlier story of my childhood pastor whose charismatic preaching and personality influenced the congregation to embrace two new real estate ventures

incoln and Mamiya, *Black Church in the African American Experience*, 175.

Closely aligned with Weber, sociologist Pierre Bourdieu argues that inherent in culture is an expression of political maneuverings within groups, reflecting their divergent interests, and that groups organize themselves in ways that minimize overt power conflicts by maximizing the political economy of "symbolic power." Bourdieu integrates the Marxian idea that symbolic systems foster the promotion of domination and class inequality, with Weber's economic model of religion to examine how language is used in religion (and other contexts) as symbolic expressions of power to establish and maintain hierarchical relations, dominance, and inequality. For Bourdieu, language is used to enable "misrecognition" of individual and/or group interests that are present in the social relations of a given social system by distracting from and/or disguising those interests, leaving others in that social system to make choices and engage in activities based on the misrecognitions. Those who promote the "misrecognition" of interests are exercising symbolic power. See Bourdieu, *Language and Symbolic Power*; Swartz, *Culture and*
; Swartz, "Bridging the Study between Culture and Religion," 71–85; Rey, "Marketing the Goods of Salvation: Bourdieu on Religion," 331–43.

despite lots of hesitation among the congregants and despite the lack of success of the previous unrealized projects.

Weber defines charisma as

> a certain quality of an individual personality by virtue of which he is set apart from ordinary men and treated as endowed with super natural, superhuman, or at least specifically exceptional powers or qualities . . . regarded as of divine origin or as exemplary, and on the basis of them, the individual concerned is treated as a leader.

Because charisma is regarded as "of divine origin," individuals and com munities tend to grant broad authority to those with exceptional qualities. In this sense, the special qualities of charisma create *de facto* privileges of their authority. The authority granted often includes decision-making and action-taking on behalf of their groups. According to Weber, charismatic individuals generally have disdain for bureaucratic processes, and as such, they are unlikely to seek endorsement before they make spe cific pronouncements or take actions.[19] After taking their actions, they use their charisma to persuade the communities to affirm the rightness of their independent actions. In this way, whether or not they intend to do so, char ismatic leaders can manipulate their communities and exert power them. As this power dynamic is engaged, the more it becomes normative, and not questioned by the communities that assent to the leaders' actions or by the leaders themselves.

In addition to the belief that the charismatic qualities are a sign of God's ordination of their leadership, the charismatic personality also cre ates within black churchgoers a strong sense of personal connection with their preachers. The personal connection and conviction that the charisma is divinely ordained, tends to make it challenging for black congregants to develop a perspective of leadership-followership that also allows for col laborative partnership with leaders that includes being able to question.

Deference to and reverence of charisma set the stage for the normal ization of a power-over dynamic between charismatic preachers and black churchgoers that disempowers black churchgoers from using and developing

---

18. Weber, *On Charisma and Institution Building*, 48.

19. Ibid., 51ff. Commenting on Weber's theory of social relations, S. N. gues that there are both creative and destructive tendencies of charisma—"on one hand, the charisma may lead to excesses of derangement and deviance, on the other hand, charismatic personalities or collectivities may be the bearers of great cultural innovations and creativity, religious, political or economic." Ibid., xx.

their own agency. The special oratorical skills and charismatic abilities of black preachers greatly contribute to a belief that pastors are uniquely gifted by God with the singular ability to know what is best for individual congregants and for the congregation as a whole. LaRue notes that the preachers most admired seem to have a natural "knack for preaching that seems more like a gift than a set of skills." Because of the oratorical skills, according to enry Mitchell, black preachers enjoy the status of being regarded "natural leaders" within the black community. As natural leaders, black preachers not only exercise the authority that is traditionally bestowed upon them, but especially demonstrate the charismatic personalities that greatly shape relations with black congregants and the larger black community.

The collective narrative that is written by charismatic leaders and their communities generally goes something like this: 1) The individual with charisma proclaims, "God has appointed me as the leader, as indicated by my exceptional qualities"; 2) The community affirms this proclamation; 3) Once agreed to, this proclamation serves as the foundation for establishing a set of rights and privileges that the leader has, including the right to make decisions on behalf of the community; 4) As the charismatic leader demonstrates his or her exceptional qualities and skills, the community forms a strong sense of personal bond with their leader, and tends not to question how things are done or explore other ways things might be done; 5) If a question is raised or suggestion made about another way to move forward, the charismatic leader tends to convey a message, directly or indirectly, "To question me, is to ques-

6) Others in the community might participate with the leader in reinforcing acquiescence as the acceptable norm; and 7) Questions and challenges from the community are silenced, and a power-over relationship between preacher and congregation is further solidified.

There are also sociological and psychological factors that foster a higher likelihood for individuals and groups to defer to charisma. S.N. isenstadt suggests that there is a "liberating power of charisma." The creativity and freedom expressed by charismatic leaders inspires a vicarious sense of liberation for individuals whose lives feel bounded in one way or other. The yearning to experience this kind of liberation often keeps followers in a loyal, unquestioning connection to charismatic leaders.

istorical experiences of racial oppression have greatly added to the development of this kind of power-over narrative as normative in black

As Weber alleges, the tendency to follow a charismatic leader emerges from experiences of "suffering, conflicts, or enthusiasm in times of

psychic, physical, economic, ethical, religious, political distress."
social oppression makes adherence to authority more likely to be perceived as a vital resource for strengthening individual and group survival, op pressed individuals and groups are also more likely to believe that following and obeying their charismatic leader is the path God has ordained for their welfare. The impact of racism on the shaping of charisma in black churches will be explored more fully in chapter 2, "The Context of Power."

The intersection of authority and charisma deepens the trust black churchgoers give to preachers and greatly heightens the degree of difficulty to question, challenge or defy their word.

## Trust and Trustworthiness

The third element of power, *trust*, is a confidence in someone's words and actions as reliable and dependable, without question or doubt, based on that person's past actions and expressed intentions. According to social ethicist Trudy Govier, trust shapes our basic conception of human nature and of the world in which we live, and it is based in the beliefs derived from a combination of our own direct experience, the experience of oth ers, and our intuitions.[21]

Not only does trust shape our conceptions of human nature, it also shapes our spiritual lives. Trust is a vital resource to helping individuals and communities to learn, heal, and grow as their trust in spiritual lead ers enables them to connect with spiritual possibilities that they might not have been able to recognize or imagine by themselves.

For many Christians, being able to trust in our spiritual leaders helps us to deepen our trust in God. For Christian social ethicist Traci C. West, the underlying reason people seek out and open themselves to ministers is a fundamental belief in the trustworthiness and integrity of ministers. Assuming that ministers have an especially strong commitment and con nection to God, churchgoers often mark their ministers as "the trustworthy center of their own Christian faith."[22] Because of the power of trust in our ministers to shape our lives, there is a power differential inherent in the clergy-congregant relationships. Therefore, assessing trustworthiness is vital to spiritual liberation.

20. Weber, *Theory of Social and Economic Organization*, 333.
21. Govier, *Dilemmas of Trust*, 6.
22. Ibid.

Catholic ethicist Richard M. Gula contends that ministers cannot be effective in ministry without being trustworthy because of the covenantal action of both giving and receiving which makes up the pastoral relationship, especially given the intrinsic inequality in power.[23] This covenantal relationship underscores the critical fiduciary responsibility and ethical demands to which the minister is divinely called to respond.

Govier argues that because trust "is an attitude that affects our emotions, beliefs, actions, and interpretations, trust involves vulnerability to This largely uni-directional vulnerability to harm establishes a power dynamic in the clergy-congregant relationship that must not be overlooked. West contends that when trust is placed in ministers, it represents the significant degree of power that clergy are given solely based upon the faith-related nature of their role as ministers.[25] Trust exponentially deepens and expands the authority that comes with the ministerial office.

With trust, congregants allow themselves to be open and vulnerable to their ministers based on qualities they perceive about their ministers over time and experience. Black churchgoers, however, are often taught to conflate and confuse trust with authority and charisma. When black churchgoers conflate these concepts, they tend to extend trust prematurely because there has not yet been a pattern of actions on the part of the leader to establish that the leader's words and actions are reliable. Or, as in the enry Lyons, even in light of evidence of significant breaches of trust by ministers, black congregants often continue deem their ministers to be trustworthy. The socialization in black churches for trust, authority and charisma to be conflated sets the stage for abuses of ministerial power as well as an underdevelopment of individual power and agency of black churchgoers—whether or not intended.

Congregational trust is supported by particular theological perspectives that regard unquestioning trust in pastors as part of spiritual practice and obligation of Christians who are mature in their faith. Because of these conventional understandings about trust, black churchgoers are often less likely to recognize when preachers are promoting the realization of their own wills. If they do recognize their preacher's promotion of his or her own will, black congregants are still less likely to resist or challenge these actions because they believe that their minister's intentions are on behalf of the

*Ethics in Pastoral Ministry*, 47.

9.

West, "Space for Faith, Sexual Desire, and Ethical Black Ministerial Practices," 43.

good of individuals or the entire congregation. Others may fear that having anything less than unquestioning trust is a sign of spiritual weakness and unwillingness to be fully surrendered to God. As a result, trust can be used as a non-coercive resource for social control.

As West notes, there is an established norm within black church cul ture for ministers to be treated as trustworthy, even if they violate people and abuse their power.[26] For West, there is a prevailing message in Christian churches in the U.S., including black churches, that suggests that the inter ests of the denominational institutions and clergy are significantly more important than the interests of congregants.[27] West also notes that while there is a critical need for establishing agreed upon standards for profes sional conduct, the high degree of trust, the sense of entitlement presumed as inherent aspects of ministry, along with high needs for power and status present among black male clergy continue to make it extremely difficult to develop such professional standards.[28]

Christian ethicist Marcia Riggs also examines how church cultures and ecclesial systems which favor ministers, especially males, above con gregants sets the stage for breaches for trust and abuses of ministerial power. Riggs, from a womanist critique of clergy power, argues that sexual-gender[29] injustice emerges from ecclesial systems that regard power as a commodity to be possessed, and thus fosters the normalization of imbal ances of power and its oppressive uses.[30]

Often in cases of clergy misconduct the primary focus is on the indi vidual pastor and any individuals who were directly abused, overlooking the breach of trust to the entire congregation. This is done with the goal of maintaining the unity of the church community because the unity and effectiveness of the community is generally associated with the reputation and credibility of the minister. As a consequence, the harm to individuals who are injured either directly or indirectly by the abuse is often dismissed as "collateral damage."[31] This approach also overlooks how the ecclesial

26. West, "Space for Faith," 44.

27. Ibid.

28. Ibid.

29. Riggs uses the term "sexual-gender" to reflect the relationships between men and women based on biological differences (sexual) and the socially constructed meanings of male and female (gender). Riggs, *Plenty Good Room*, 21.

30. Ibid., 104.

31. Lebacqz and Barton, *Ethics and Spiritual Care*, 229.

system, by its protection of clergy, contributes to the fostering of a church culture where abuses of power are accepted and normalized.

In historically black church contexts where theology, training, and socialization support trusting ministers, whether or not warranted, leaves the hearts and minds of black congregants open to "greater vulnerability to harm." Given that trust is extended by the congregants to clergy often automatically, at times unconsciously, and especially when individuals are in crisis or distress, clergy have critical fiduciary responsibility to counter-balance the power relations at work in the intersection of trust, authority, and charisma. Without conscious focus on the fiduciary responsibility of trustworthiness, clergy can begin to "believe their own press"—that is, be-lieve that their authority received from church officials, charisma endowed by God, and trust extended by congregants are signs of their inalienable and irrevocable rights, privileges, and power over their congregants.

## Clergy Authority and Pyramidal Power

The combination of authority bestowed upon clergy by ecclesiastical man-date of apostolic succession, the deference given to charismatic gifts as a leadership seal of approval from God, along with the perspective that obedience and trust foster unity in a church community together lay the foundations for clergy-congregant relationships reflective of a power-*over* pyramidal paradigm. To a large extent, this power-*over* paradigm has run throughout the history of black denominational churches.

Psychologist Leonard Doob outlines the foundations for pyramidal power, in his definition of power as

> the actual or potential ability of one or more participants (or forces), *according to the true or false conviction* of an observer or a participant, to have affected or to affect the specified, significant actions of one or more other participants (or forces)."[32]

Power, in this sense, is not based on pre-ordained hierarchical relation-ships, but on the convictions, perceptions, or beliefs of observers—whether or not the basis of these convictions, perceptions, and beliefs is valid. While hierarchical relationships are not required for the existence and exercise of power, according to Doob, hierarchy gives greater import to authority. Hi-erarchy emphasizes authority by: (1) "the repeated, true or false conviction

*Personality, Power, and Authority,* 8.

that the hierarchical *position*" of the leader can affect the actions of others, (2) leaders serving as the *reference point* for that conviction, and ( gaining the *consent* of the one or more individuals whose specific actions and life choices are affected by their leaders.[33]

Institutionally-sanctioned hierarchies intersect with authority, cha risma, and trust to reinforce a conviction within the followers that their leaders have the abilities and God-ordained rights to affect their actions, their lives, and even their salvation. As this conviction becomes internal ized, churchgoers become less likely to explore their own human agency— that is, their own innate power to affect their own lives—but instead, tend to rely more upon the direction of their leaders. The community itself plays a vital role in fostering traditional ways of relating to its leaders that are often passed down through generations. Because of the power positions they have in the hierarchy, however, black ministers can either further per petuate traditional ways of relating that black congregants may engage in that are familiar to them, or ministers can assist black churchgoers in creat ing new visions for clergy-congregant relationships based in paradigms of mutual empowerment and liberation .

I am not suggesting that all hierarchy is bad and to be avoided. What I am saying, however, is that black preachers, who are intentionally commit ted to the supporting the empowerment of black Christians and all other blacks, must be aware of and counter-balance for the kinds of power-over dynamics often present in church hierarchies.

The three interlocking elements of power—authority, charisma, and trust—contribute to the creation and maintenance of clergy-congregant relationships that are what Du Bois refers to as "a reproduced microcosm" of the very kind of hierarchical and exclusionary power relations in the broader U.S. society that marginalize blacks. They also work together in ways that keep the scope of ministerial authority either too broad or too nebulous, thus making black churches contexts that are often ripe for both abuses of ministerial power and the disempowerment of churchgoers.
ism has greatly influenced both the theology of the preacher's role and the association of community's survival with the authority of the preacher.

While none of these aspects of power is exclusive to black church com munities, the particular expressions of each of these elements and their inter sections are demonstrated in ways uniquely shaped by the black experience in America. How these elements of social power—authority, charisma, and

33. Ibid., 8–9.

trust—are distinctively present in black denominational churches emerging from the impacts of racial oppression are the focus of this next chapter.

## 2

# The Nexus of Racism and Power

The Preacher is the most unique personality *developed by the Negro* can soil. A leader, a politician, an orator, a "boss," an intriguer, and idealist.

ANTI-BLACK RACISM HAS CARVED a distinctive role for black ministers in their relationships with congregants, as they have served in mul tiple roles as spiritual leaders, representatives of black communities, monitors of social control, and as mediators/interpreters of ideologies from the broader society. Within black communities and in the larger white-dominated public sphere, black preachers historically have been highly regarded as the leaders and community spokespersons for blacks in America. Anti-black racism shapes the ways that the power trinity of authority, charisma, and trust are expressed in the relationships be tween black preachers and their congregants.

Despite some significant changes in the broader U.S. society and the experiences of blacks within the society, the role of black preachers has re mained largely unchanged since the formation of historically black church denominations. What are the factors in the initial shaping of this role that continue to give it such strong force in the lives of black Christians today? Is this the most effective role in furthering the quest for the liberation of African Americans today?

1. Du Bois, "Souls of Black Folk" in *Writings*, 494. Emphasis added.

## Preacher Power in the Formative Black Church

Some of the elements of the power of black preachers *over* the lives of their congregants emerge from the religious life that slaves brought with them frica, adapted in slavery and to the Christian instruction given to slaves by white preachers. For example, W. E. B. Du Bois contends that the centrality of religion and the power of the medicine man or priest in the lives of blacks were two aspects of African culture African slaves brought with merica. These two cultural realities greatly contributed to the relative power of black preachers as developed on American soil. He argues,

> Based in a theo-cultural understanding of the role of their priests as representatives of their West African religions, African slaves tended to project onto their black preachers the power to interpret the supernatural, comfort them in their sorrow, and to speak on their behalf to white slaveowners.[2]

Cleophus LaRue also posits that the authority and trust given generously to black preachers originated in the religious cultures of West Africa, where the priests and medicine men were bestowed high degrees of authority, respect and admiration because of the importance ascribed to their tribal roles. This high regard was then transferred to the slave preachers' role.[3]

nlike other work functions carried out in their role as slaves, the function of preachers was generally not in the service of, for the profit of, nor under the direct control of whites. As such, this role gave preachers considerably greater freedom and more power relative to other slaves. In his study of black religion during slavery, Albert Raboteau notes that the relative degree of power and authority emerging from the preacher function was not welcomed by all whites for it was considered to open a space for slaves to experience a sphere of freedom independent from direct white control.[4] In a denominational magazine in the mid-19th century, Episcopalians opined,

> We look upon the habit of Negro preaching as a wide-spreading evil; not because a black man cannot be a good [preacher], but . . . because they acquire an influence independent of the owner, and not subject to his control . . . when they have possessed this power, they have been known to make an improper use of it.[5]

113.

*Heart of Black Preaching* 12.

aboteau, *Slave Religion*, 179–80.

Ibid. See footnote 54, quoting Hayden, "Conversion and Control: Dilemma of

Black congregations developed during slavery (predominately Baptist, Methodist, Presbyterian, and Episcopal) under the ecclesial control of and close surveillance by white congregations. While there was an expressed goal of missionaries from the various denominations to promote the Christianization and salvation of black slaves, the sentiment was also understood that the property interests that slave-owners held in those slaves was to be preserved. These spiritual and economic issues were held in a precarious balance. Christianizing the black slaves served as a tool of oppression and control of black masses, but also served as a resource for the seeds of liberation for slaves, especially slave preachers.

Despite a measure of surveillance[6] that black congregations endured, preachers still had a relatively high degree of autonomy, including in relation to their work function as slaves for they would be given a measure of latitude with their slave work to attend to the spiritual needs of their congregations. According to E. Franklin Frazier, because of the relative autonomy of slave preachers and the absence of an established priesthood for slaves, preachers played an important role in the development of the "invisible institution" of the slave church even in a social context where slaves were forbidden to organize social efforts.[7] With the leverage and social capital of this role, slave preachers "achieved a position of dominance."

In his critique of slave preachers, Frazier alleges that the preachers played critical roles in social control. The pattern of control and organization within the black churches was "authoritarian, with a strong man in a dominant position As a consequence, Negroes have had little education in democratic processes."[9]

As a departure from an earlier "spirit of revolt' and resistance among black slaves who embraced Christianity, Du Bois contends that by the mid-nineteenth century many slaves had become "unconsciously ripe for a new philosophy of life the doctrines of passive submission embodied in the new newly learned Christianity."[10] From this context of "passive submission"

---

Episcopalians in Providing for the Religious Instructions of Slave, Charleston, South Carolina, 1845–1860," 143.

6. Foucault discusses the power of surveillance to keep people within the prescribed parameters of a particular society or group. See Foucault, *Power/Knowledge*

7. Frazier, *Negro Church in America*, 17.

8. Ibid., citing Frederick Douglass, "the preacher was one of the slave notabilities." See Douglass, *Life and Times of Frederick Douglass*, 31.

9. Ibid., 85–86.

10. Du Bois, "Souls of Black Folk" in *Writings*, 499.

emerged the black male preacher. The power-over, dominant relations present in the broader society between slave owners and slaves set the stage for the power relations re-produced in the black church between black preachers and congregants.

Du Bois also argues that because of the long-term socialization of submission emerging from slavery, black Christians were ripe for an excessive sway of their preachers functioning as *candidates for power*. Influenced by both the demoralization of slavery and a theo-cultural need to regard black preachers as powerful, participants in the early formation of black churches, in the midst of their "longing and disappointment and resentment," gave authority to black male ministers to direct their lives in ways that are distinctive to the black Christian experience in the U.S.[11] Black Christians—clergy and laity alike—according to Du Bois, "put an undue premium upon finesse and personal influence,"[12] as they regarded their preachers in multiple roles as leaders, politicians, orators, and bosses. In this context, black preachers served as the "reference point"[13] for how black slaves could live, or imagine living their lives.

## The Impact of Oppression on Black Preaching

The formational experience of the Christian religion in the U.S. was laced with strong anti-black racism, black Christians have had to navigate two sets of forces—their own religious sensibilities and the directives from the white church.

In his report, *The Negro Church* in 1903, Du Bois highlight three key points about the social context of the African American. Namely, Du Bois          ) the use of the religious instruction to keep African slaves obedient to their slave masters, 2) the legal prohibition against blacks' use of their church assembly as occasions to plan revolts, and 3) the indoctrina-frican slaves to believe that slavery was their pathway for salvation of their souls. Below are brief examples of each of these formative influences upon the black Christians.

Du Bois, "The New Negro Church" in *Against Racism*, 113.
    45. Emphasis added.
    *Personality Power and Authority*, 8–9.

*Religious Instruction:*

> There was one hard doctrine to which we as slaves were compelled
> to listen . . . We were often told by the ministers how much we owed
> to God for bringing us over from the benighted shores of
> . . . There was one [ ] clergyman [who] preached a sermon to us in
> which he urged from the Bible that it was the will of heaven from all
> eternity that we should be slaves, and our masters be our owners.

*Legal Prohibition Influence:*

> Maryland passed a law in 1723 to suppress tumultuous meetings
> of slaves on Sabbath and other holy days, 'a measure primarily for
> good order, but also tending to curb independent religious meetings
> among Negroes . . . Georgia in 1770 forbade slaves "to assemble on
> pretense of feasting,' etc., and . . . every slave which may be found
> at such meeting, as aforesaid, shall . . . immediately be corrected,
> without trial, by receiving on the bare back twenty-five stripes.

*Indoctrination Regarding Slavery as the Salvific Plan of God*
As reflected in this testimony of a black Methodist minister:

> . . . I am now induced to think God may have a higher end in per
> mitting them to be brought to this Christian country, than mere
> ly to support their masters. Many of the poor slaves in
> have already been made freemen of the heavenly Jerusalem and
> possibly a time may come when many thousands may embrace
> the gospel, and thereby be brought into the glorious liberty of the
> children of God.[16]

This racist social context, Du Bois argues, directs blacks to perceive them
selves only through the lens of the cultural, political, and theological he
gemony. Black preachers, even with spiritual anointing and charisma, are
not immune to the effects of the cultural trauma[17] of racism. As such, the
effects of racist traumatization manifest in black preachers and what they
preach. The impact is reflected in collective memory, double conscious
ness, and dialectic tensions transmitted through black preaching.

14. Du Bois, "Negro Church," 29–30, citing Bassett, *State*, 51–52.

15. Ibid., 11, citing *Prince's Digest*, 447.

16. Ibid., 10.

17. Ron Eyerman argues, "The notion of cultural trauma implies that direct experi
ence of an event is not a necessary condition for its inclusion in the traumatic process. It
is through time-delayed and negotiated recollection that cultural trauma is experienced."
Eyerman, *Cultural Trauma: Slavery and the Formation of African American Identity*

Sociologist Ron Eyerman defines "collective memory" as recollections of "a shared past that are handed down generation to generation in an ongoing process.[18] Both group identity and individual identity are shaped by and negotiated within the collective memory. For that reason collective memory becomes a social necessity for both the individuals within the group as well as the group as a whole.

Without the sense of rooting that a collective memory can serve to offer, the identities of both the group and the individuals become too uncertain. Without a strong sense of identity, navigating the world becomes too danger-

*Interpretations* of past events become as important, if not more than, the past events in shaping the understandings of current experiences of blacks. Thus, whoever has the "power of telling" or gatekeeping the collective narrative plays a critical and powerful role in the identity formation of both the group and the individual members of the group.

Serving historically as the mediators/interpreters for black communities, black preachers have played a powerful role as the gatekeepers of the black collective memory, especially for black Christians. Black preachers have shaped the meaning of specific events that have happened in the collective life of African Americans. Across the generations, black preachers have been the preeminent interpreters of the cultural traumas of slavery, Reconstruction, Jim Crowism, and contemporary expressions of racism, and have served as the reference points for how to navigate the broader society.

1903 seminal work, *The Souls of Black Folk*, Du Bois frames the experiences of black Americans as born into a racist social context which limits their ability to develop a self-consciousness primarily based on their own self-identification and self-definition. "Such a double life," Du Bois argues, "with double thoughts, double duties, and double social classes, must give rise to double words and double ideals, and tempt the mind to pretence or revolt, to hypocrisy or radicalism."[19] This double consciousness runs as a thread in black preaching bringing two sets of messages about how to navigate in the society—one that is liberative, and the other constrictive. One that inspires black churchgoers to live guided by their own spiritual authority, and the other that conveys to them that they need preachers to tell them how to live. According to Du Bois,

> It is such incessant self-questioning and the hesitation that arises from it, that is making the present period a time for vacillation

6.

Du Bois, "Souls of Black Folk," in *Writings*, 502.

and contradiction for the American Negro; combined race action is stifled, race responsibility is shirked, race enterprises languish, and the best energy of the Negro people cannot be marshaled to do the bidding of the race.[20]

Because of the inner wrestling within African Americans' race identity con sciousness, blacks are 1) stuck in vacillation, 2) stifled in the collective action, 3) shirking in their race responsibility, 4) unable to sustain productive busi nesses and initiatives, and 5) emotionally and spiritually drained.

quality of dualistic disempowerment reflected in black preaching today?

Lincoln and Mamiya assert that sermon content may be one of the most revealing indicators of black consciousness.[21] In their of 2,150 preachers, Lincoln and Mamiya observe deep-seated, race-based inferiority reflected in the sermons of a majority of African preachers. Their research revealed variations in black clergy's perspectives on black consciousness based on age, education, and denomination (with age and education as the strongest variables).[22] For example, as they note, 79.4 per cent of clergy under the age of 40 tended to include race-affirming messages in their sermons, whereas only 53 per cent of those who were over the age of sixty included such messages in their preaching.

> As our study has shown, the influence of black consciousness upon the black clergy and their churches has had mixed results. While the majority of black clergy have tended to put more em phasis upon their denomination's historical heritage, black pride, the need for black role models in Sunday School literature, and a more unique sense of how black churches differ from others, most of them have not been influenced by the new movement of black liberation theology.[23]

While we cannot be certain what the trends are today, twenty years after the Lincoln and Mamiya study, because shifts in group consciousness are slow moving, it is reasonable to believe that how race consciousness is presented in sermons today probably does not reflect a significant change.

20. Du Bois, "The Conservation of Races" in *Writings*, 821.

21. Lincoln and Mamiya, *Black Church in the African American Experience* see the Introduction of this paper, where I proposed four basic sermon themes—Spiritual Authority, Individual Victories, Afterlife Freedom, and God's Justice—that impact both worshipers' self-identity and their understanding of who God is.

22. Ibid., 176.

23. Ibid., 195.

If much of the emphasis is still on the distinctiveness of denominational heritage as a measure of black consciousness, the question must be raised about whether denominational heritage serves to mobilize black churchgoers as collaborators with God in healing the world.

incoln and Mamiya also conclude that black churches and preachers are caught in an ongoing series of dialectical tensions.[24] This pattern of dialectic tension is reflected in a common tendency among many black preachers to avoid issues of racial consciousness in their sermons. Informed by Du Bois' theory of double-consciousness, Lincoln and Mamiya proffer an interpretive schema which reflects six dialectic tensions within the black church and black preaching. The Lincoln and Mamiya schema is useful in fostering an understanding of the dichotomies perceivable in black churches, representing the major theological, ecclesiastical, social, and political themes commonly reflected in black sermons. The six dialectic pairs that they propose: 1) *Priestly and Prophetic*; 2) *Other-Worldly and This-Worldly*; *Universalism and Particularism*; 4) *Communal and Privatistic*; 5) *Charismatic and Bureaucratic*; and 6) *Resistance and Accommodation*.[25]

incoln and Mamiya argue that due to the presence of these dialectic tensions, the effectiveness of many black churches as a liberative force in the merican community is constrained. While their study addresses the content of black sermons, it focuses solely on the ways in which black preachers address the issues of racial identity and racism in the U.S., and leaves largely unaddressed the dichotomies *within* black churches relating to issues of power relations. Nonetheless, this dialectic schema will be useful in helping us understand what contributes to the messages about social power in the sermons used for our analysis.

ccording to Christian ethicist Peter Paris, black sermons give their attention almost exclusively to a reliance on God's power, and ignore what black Christians can do themselves using their own personal and collective agency to bring about needed social changes.[26] Failure to emphasize the personal agency of black Christians, Paris argues, limits the sense of freedom and independence available through the black church experience to the confines of black church buildings and does not substantively foster the degree of empowerment needed to express this freedom in the broader, racist society.[27] That is, although black churchgoers may experience a sense

11.

incoln and Mamiya, *Black Church in the African American Experience*, 12ff.

*Social Teaching of the Black Churches*, 94–95.

95.

of emotional freedom while gathered together as a congregation, the emo
tionally freeing worship experience does not sufficiently equip them with a
sense of empowerment that strengthens their individual ethical agency in
society nor sufficiently challenge them to engage their moral authority for
social justice activism.

## The "Curriculum Effect"

Many black churchgoers are socialized to accept power-*over*
gregant relationships as normative, perhaps even divinely mandated.
pyramidal clergy-congregant relationships are so normative that for black
male preachers to lead a charge in examining and critiquing the power
relations within the black church, they may risk ostracism if regarded as
attempting to dismantle a tradition of black male clergy power—a social
power not as readily available to them elsewhere in U.S. society.
sequence, the system of charismatic preacher "at the top" of the social or
der with power-*over* has remained strongly intact. Black churchgoers are
taught that to be good Christians and live in "the perfect will of the
they must help maintain that social order.

Reflecting on her experience as a schoolteacher working with black
second-grade students, Patricia Hill Collins observes, "so many have been
silenced by classroom practices that rewarded their obedience and punished
their curiosity that they were justifiably afraid to question the public tran
script known as their curriculum."[28] While many blacks and others may tend
to regard this kind of "curriculum-effect" as happening upon black children
and adults only at the hands of hegemonic forces in the dominant
there are also traditions within black communities, including black churches
which participate in promulgating particular "curricula" that constrict the
sense of human efficacy and moral agency of blacks. The curriculum influ
ences *within* black churches silence the voices and reward the acquiescence
of black Christians—adults and children, female and male, clergy and laity.
As such, the curriculum fosters the internalization of what Paris calls "an
ambiguous social ethic" that has both a liberating and limiting effect.

First, as Du Bois observes blacks learn to express a sense of their pow
er in the black church community, only to return to "the other world which
does not know and does not want to know [their] power."[29]

28. Collins, *Fighting Words*, x.
29. Du Bois, "Souls of Black Folk," 369–70.

social reality, messages that are diluted by dialectic tensions—such as, "You are powerful, but only to the extent that the preacher tells you that you are, or not as powerful as the pastor" serve to foster an ambiguous social ethic that disempowers black Christians.

Second, social theorist John McWhorter contends that there is a specific expression of double-consciousness among many black Americans today that manifests as an emphasis on "personal initiative and strength in private but dutifully takes on the mantle of victimhood in public."[30] Because dichotomous messages about power heard and experienced in the black churches often maintain the preacher's power-over the congregants, as in the case of my childhood church, congregants may "speak their minds" privately, but are often less inclined to challenge those "in authority." Thus, black churches have become training grounds for socializing black Christians to wear the mantle of "public victim" in power relations. At times, the mantle of victim might not be overt, but may be expressed in passive-aggressive ways toward those who are perceived to "be in charge" or aggressiveness and "throwing their weight around" in relation to those not perceived to be in charge.

Third, the combination of double-consciousness and a sinfulness-based theology framed by the dialectic tensions present in sermons greatly contribute to an ambiguous self-esteem. Ambiguous self-esteem, in turn, influences how blacks relate in aspects of their lives, including socio-po-ccording to political science professor and news commentator arris-Lacewell,

> The content of the spiritual advice [the black church] gives can shape the political perspectives of those who receive it . . . and contributes to the psychological resources, such as self esteem and internal efficacy that encourage black churchgoers to engage with politics.[31]

Sermons are a form of "advice-giving" that boast unparalled import and influence as "the word of God."[32] Words that might otherwise be construed as advice or guides to live by are often instead framed as directives from God by which churchgoers are mandated, or at least expected, to arris-Lacewell rightly centralizes the impact of the "psychological

McWhorter, "Double Consciousness in Black America," 14–15, 1.

arris-Lacewell, *Barbershops, Bibles, and BET*, 8.

Black preachers are traditionally regarded as special representative or ambassadors of God and their preaching is commonly regarded as "the word of God" consistent with the biblical prophetic claim, "thus saith the Lord." This concept is explored more fully in chap-as part of a discussion on the three elements of power—authority, charisma, and trust.

resources" of "self esteem and internal efficacy" for how black Christians engage in the politics. The ethical focus here is not solely on black participation in the political electoral process, but more on the understandings of power relations that undergird how black churchgoers engage in the broader culture sociopolitically.

In this way, the dialectic tensions and training for victimhood present in black sermons serve to perpetuate messages from the broader society that undercut the self-esteem of blacks. As a consequence, black churchgoers are often far less empowered and have lower self-esteem than their black counterparts who do not attend church.

Despite the tenacious hold of this power norm, as Lincoln and Mamiya's observation suggests, even the pyramidal power relations that place black male pastors at the top of the power ladder still do not develop the stronger sense of selfhood even for those who are at the top of the church hierarchy. Because the black preaching tradition and church structure have not helped develop a strong sense of self or needed "psychological resources" within black preachers, they are more likely to employ domination and control as symbolic representations of their self-esteem, often not affirmed in the dominant society.

Because these symbolic representations cannot meet the underlying psychological need for high self-esteem, however, especially among black male clergy for whom authoritarian leadership is associated with a sense of personal importance, or "somebodiness," many are likely to hold tenaciously to the symbol of their selfhood in ways that impede the true experience of selfhood and empowerment not only for themselves, but also for black churchgoers. As gatekeepers of the collective memory, and thus the group identity of black church community, there is a tendency for black male preachers in particular to use their gatekeeping role in ways that serve their self-interests. The consequence is an underdevelopment of the full power of all Christians.

Because of the unconditional trust that congregants often extend to the pastors, congregants are likely to associate their pastors' authoritarian control and domination with the "leading of the Holy Spirit" to address some area of their lives in which they need to be humbled and become more obedient and conformable to the Spirit. It is in such contexts that congregants, even when ministers betray congregational trust and abuse ministerial power, do not hold their pastors accountable, but rather are more likely to engage of the common strategies outlined by ethicist Marie

Fortune: villainize the whistleblower, misname the problem, or blame the

In short, because of the curriculum effect, black churchgoers, as reflected in the story of Henry Lyons, tend to find ways to defend or overlook the pastors' words and actions.

mong black churchgoers, the implications of the curriculum effect are strong for a few key reasons: (1) an association of the spiritual leader with a sense of survival, (2) a learned passive submission, and (3) a presumption that imbalance of power is worth the risks.

First, the ambassadorial role that black preachers have historically played in relating to the larger white society on behalf of blacks fostered not only the survival of blacks, but also bolstered within blacks a sense of confidence, reliance, and trust in black male preachers as their "natural leaders." Black congregants often associate, not only their survival, but also their success with the overall success of their preachers in navigating through the social, political, educational, and economic waters of the wider U.S. society.

istorically, black preachers have served as barometers of what advances are possible in the wider society for their congregants.[34]

Second, the passive submission described by Du Bois as emanating from the socialization during slavery and subsequent racial oppression established a tradition of deference given to "those in authority" that has been handed down through the generations. This learned passive submission that has been part of the black church origins and tradition amplifies the significance and weight of the theology of ministerial authority through apostolic succession, examined by Campenhausen. Because of the nexus of social oppression and theological formation, being in alignment with ministerial authority has often held a heightened position in the spiritual

.S. black Christians and the role of apostolic succession as the

Fortune, *Is Nothing Sacred?*, 120–22.

For example, within black church folklore, it has commonly been assumed that the preacher would be first in the church to get certain automobiles that represent upward socio-economic status—a Cadillac during the 1960–80s, a Mercedes-Benz in the

s, and a Rolls Royce in this current era. Another critical symbol of moving beyond mere survival toward success is academic degrees. Preachers, as seen in black church custom, are also generally the first to acquire academic degrees. Because of this badge of success, a common honorific reference extended to well-respected black male pastors is "Doc," whether or not they have engaged in doctoral studies, or even matriculated in a college. In my lifetime of association with black churches, while I have heard numerous black male preachers referred to as "Doc," I have never heard one woman referenced by this titular signature of respect, except those who have actually earned doctoral degrees, and even then this title is used sparingly.

determinant of ministerial authority has played and continues to play a major role in the contemporary black church.[35]

Third, Mitchell observes, "Black preachers, like any others, risk pomposity when they assume roles in their speaking—like the role of God or of some other character or spectator in a Bible narrative—but the role carefully portrayed is a tremendous asset to preaching."[36] comments suggests, while there is a level of recognition about the status of black male preachers at the top of the church power pyramid, because the overall preaching function is regarded so highly, the benefits are presumed to be worth the potential risks and costs. While Mitchell's comment reflects recognition of the moral risk to individual preachers, there are also critical risk and costs to the moral and ethical development of the black church community and beyond.

## Epistemological Tradition in Black Churches

Historically black preachers have served as interpreters not only of Christian scripture, but also of black experience in the U.S. society and overall life experience. As black Christians have been taught not to look behind and under "the sacred desk" to discern what curriculum or interpretive influences there are that shape their preachers and what they preach. They

35. This reference is more commonly used in African Methodist E Methodist Episcopal Zion, and Christian Methodist Episcopal churches, and also applies to historically black congregations within predominantly white denominations, such as United Church of Christ and Presbyterian Church (U.S.A). There are three different categories of titular honorifics regarding the ministerial office which reflect the significance of apostolic succession. One, in denominations where ministers are appointed to local congregations, pastors are more likely referred to as "reverend." Two, in the various Baptist conventions, while most pastors are referred to as "reverend" or "pastor," there is also a growing movement for fellowships of churches to affirm a charismatic, luminary preacher as "bishop." See for example, pastors of Baptist megachurches such as Bishop Eddie Long (see later in this study), Bishop Paul Morton (Full Gospel Baptist Church Fellowship), Bishop Walter Thomas (New Psalmist Baptist Church), and Bishop Walker (Love Fellowship). For example, speaking of an upcoming "public affirmation" of Frederick K. Price to the position of "Apostle of Faith," Bishop Harry Jackson notes, "While Paul did not walk with Jesus, when Jesus appointed him apostle, Paul became a preview of that which was to come." Spirit of Faith Christian Center (Dr. Mike Freeman, Maryland) television broadcast, aired on Word Network, May 20, 2008 ture is designed to connote a direct line of authority originating with Jesus Christ, to the early church apostles, and through the ages to contemporary apostles.

36. Mitchell, *Black Preaching*, 168.

have been taught to regard all that their preachers preach and teach as "a word from the Lord." The black church curriculum has taught that all of what preachers know is revealed to them by God. In this way, many black churchgoers treat the preached word almost as if it were untouched and un-tainted by the knowledge, experiences, and the psychological resources that preachers bring to "the word." The tendency to approach the preached word as untouched and untainted by preachers' lives, as "buildings not made with hands" is influenced by the theology of apostolic succession that suggests that God speaks directly and exclusively to those who are appointed and anointed by God as spiritual leaders.

What are the "givens"—those teachings, systems, and structures that have been culturally prescribed as "immutable truth" for black Christians—that have been spoken from behind "the sacred desk" that are not to be questioned or challenged? Is "a word from the Lord" the only basis of what black preachers know and how they interpret life? These questions invite black churchgoers to explore all of the theological, cultural, and personal resources of information that shape what preachers know and what they preach and teach.

*Epistemology* is the study of what we know and how we acquire that knowledge. Being shaped in a social context where issues of theology, power, and racism intersect, what black preachers (and churchgoers) know is influenced by all three of these factors, independently and interdependently. To treat what black preachers know as only acquired from the Spirit leaves out important dimensions of what is preached and why it is preached.

s ethicist Ivone Gebara contends, "all epistemologies lead us to ethi-
Therefore, to explore the conceptual and interpretive systems of the black church tradition is also to investigate the ethical formation of black Christians. Exploring issues of epistemology becomes an important resource for understanding and interrupting how power structures func-tion and how they continue to propagate themselves through the knowl-edge that is transmitted.

The nexus of socialization in the U.S. race-based caste system and the black church curriculum laced with double consciousness have been and continue to be the norms of a conceptual system that greatly influences black preaching. To help provide a framework for examining how this intersection is reflected in black sermons, the next chapter provides an interdisciplinary analytical framework required for a comprehensive interrogation of black sermons and the socioethical implications flowing from them.

Gebara, *Longing for Running Water*, 23.

# 3

## Critical Approaches to Sermon Analysis

The colored world therefore must be seen as existing not simply for itself but as a group whose insistent cry may yet become the warning which awakens the world to its truer self and its wider destiny.[1]

ASSUMPTIONS ABOUT POWER RELATIONS are imbedded in the liturgical language used in sermons and other aspects of the worship experience, whether or not they are consciously engaged by black preachers and churchgoers. The assumptions about power, "encoded in liturgical language,"[2] especially relate to race, class, and gender. Because the assumptions embedded in church language become normative, as a consequence of consistent use and expressions of church culture, they can often go unrecognized and unquestioned.

*Hermeneutics*, the art, science and theory of interpretation of sacred/ scriptural texts, in its original use, focused on assisting audiences in determining *how to live in society*.[3] Liturgical studies scholar Joyce Zimmerman alleges that because all communication engages at least some interpretation,[4] exploring issues of interpretation is vital to any hermeneutical exploration. Although interpretation is always at work, Zimmerman

---

1. Du Bois, "Dusk of Dawn" in *Du Bois Writings*, 680.
2. Saliers, *Worship as Theology*, 140–41.
3. Zimmerman, *Liturgy and Hermeneutics*, 24.
4. Ibid., 6.

contends, interlocutors are often unaware of their own interpretive activity,[5] and tend to regard and encourage others to regard their statements as if they were facts. Therefore, because much of the interpretive work is unconscious and because of the deep impact of authority, charisma, and trust, the beliefs and worldviews held by black preachers are handed down through generations of clergy and congregants as normative and treated as fact.[6]

Sermon text analysis enables us to identify the interpretive influences acting upon both the preachers and the hearers of sermons. The work of sermon text analysis is to separate sermonic content from sermon style often deemed as traditional in order to understand the interpretive activity that is reflected in the sermons and to distinguish their historic meanings relative to their contemporary implications. Engaging in a process of contextualizing sermonic language, that is, locating homiletic traditions in their original socio-historical contexts and examining the factors that shaped those traditions enables more critical analyses of the implications of those traditions when used in contemporary contexts. Such contextualizations further assist us in assessing sermonic language in light of its expressed ideals, principles, and goals in response to contemporary needs.

Socio-historical contexts both shape and are shaped by sermonic language reflecting complex, multivalent, and interlocking theological, sociological, psychological, and political, and economic issues. Additionally, assumptions about power, gender and class are often present in the analytic methods used to explore and discuss sermons texts,[7] especially when the analyses are engaged by those for whom traditional sermonic language has become normative. To engage critical methods that expand beyond normative assumptions about power, gender, race, and class requires the integration of multivalent analytic approaches. Therefore, this chapter provides an overview of four distinctive approaches to sermon text analysis, namely: black religious hermeneutics, womanist-feminist analytic strategy, post-critical

---

Philosophy of religion professor Keith Yandell defines religious tradition as "a conceptual system that provides an interpretation of the world and the place of human beings in it, that builds on that interpretation account of how life should be lived in the world, and that expresses this interpretation and life-style in a set of rituals, institutions, and practices." Yandell, *Epistemology of Religious Experience*, 6.

140. In his presentment of liturgical language as encoded with assumptions power, class and gender, Saliers' failure to list race as an area in which assumptions are made reflects his point about how assumptions are shaped by our social locations.

hermeneutics, and sociological rhetorical criticism. These approaches will be integrated for the sermon analyses presented in later chapters.

## Black Religious Hermeneutics

Simply put, black religious hermeneutics constitutes a body of interpreta tions about the black religious experience in the U.S. This body of inter pretations, relating to black preaching, is shaped primarily by analytical approaches within homiletics and sociology. Each of these interpretive ap proaches largely frames the black religious experience—especially, worship and preaching—in terms of its response to the racial oppression that blacks experience in the broader society.

According to black homiletics scholar Henry Mitchell, the black church experience is the "unique response" of blacks to a history of racism. Black preaching, Mitchell argues, is shaped by the "sociology, economics, government, [and] culture—the total ethos—of the black ghetto" and is af fected by, produces and changes a black theology that speaks to the condi tions of blacks in America.[8]

Cleophus LaRue posits that because the hermeneutic of black preach ing emerges out of the origins of the black church during slavery and post-slavery oppression to understand the distinctiveness of the black preaching tradition necessitates an understanding of the black socio-cultural context. For LaRue, the hallmark of black preaching is the interpretive lens it pro vides to help blacks to deal with and rise above the marginalization that has been part of the historical experience of blacks in U.S.[9]

Black homiletical approaches generally focus on the theological, his torical and stylistic aspects of sermons that highlight theological and social tensions within the black Christian experience relative to the broader social context. Because of the common black hermeneutical focus on racism and its effects, analyses of black sermons have made only limited investigations

8. Mitchell, *Black Preaching*, 196.

9. Susan Bond argues that LaRue is "one of the few [black] homiletical voices calling for sustained attention to corporate and communal issues related to preaching," and who, unlike most homileticians, does not assume that all sermons within the black preaching tradition have issues of social justice as a central theme. Bond's contention that not all sermons have social justice issues as a central theme reflects a further tendency to un derstate how central the theme of social justice is in the scriptures, and to understate the responsibility of black pastors to inspire congregations to direct participation in social justice action. Bond, *Contemporary African American Preaching*, 17.

into the issues of power, class, and gender assumptions that Saliers posits are encoded in worship.[10]

nalyses of black preaching tend to focus on preparation and delivery of sermons and on how sermons provide therapeutic release and empowerment for black Christians to cope with racism and other oppressions in the broader culture.[11] For example, LaRue offers four critical elements of the black preaching hermeneutic that traditional homiletical approaches focus on: biblical scripture, lived experience,[12] demonstrations of God's power in the lives of congregants, and use of extended metaphors that point to the further possibilities of God's power at work.[13] Engaging these four elements, ue outlines several characteristics of common methodological approaches used in analyzing black preaching, including: 1) skillful articulation, 2) sense of divine encounter, 3) importance of wrestling with the text, 4) the waiting congregation, 5) astute awareness of the broader culture, 6) use of written manuscript at least for preparation, 7) attention to the closing of ser-
) continuous reflection and creation of sermons, 9) use of the poetics of hymnody, 10) disciplined study, and 11) preaching from an overflow of gathered materials.[14] These characteristics focus on preparation and delivery, and do not attend to the ethical implications of sermon content.

These hermeneutical elements, LaRue argues, represent domains of black life experiences in America—"personal piety," "care of the soul," "social justice," "corporate concerns," and "maintenance of the institutional church." Personal pietism, which stresses the centrality of scripture, morality, and the priesthood of all believers to be expressed in the personal lives of black Christians, is the most common thematic emphasis of black
Care of the soul focuses on the personal well-being, forgiveness,

lso see Bourdieu, *Language and Symbolic Power*.

ue argues that the primary goal of black sermons is to empower the community by fostering "a meaningful connection between an all-powerful God and a marginalized and powerless people" and to help the people celebrate their lives in the midst of oppression. See LaRue, *Heart of Black Preaching*, 12.

Mitchell emphasizes that there is a "ritual freedom" present in black church worship experience, facilitated by the preaching, that "mediates the love and grace of God to a race of people who have been despised and rejectedin a world of forced, hurried conformity, the Black Church remains an oasis where God and his children meet and talk to each other. 'Freedom' is the key word describing this experience Nobody is under pressure." Mitchell, 47.

ue, *Heart of Black Preaching*, 24.

ue, *Power in the Pulpit*, 3ff.

ue, *Heart of Black Preaching*, 24.

and renewal. Social justice, the third domain, emphasizes that God is both the source of all social justice and that God's power enables black Christians to bring needed social reforms. Unlike the focus of social justice on the common good, corporate concerns center exclusively on the needs and in terests of black Americans. Maintenance of the institutional church, contends, is "more concerned with ethos than specific acts" that present God's power as made more visible in the life of the faith community.

By focusing on how black church communities respond to God at work in their lives and to racism in the larger society, with limited excep tion, homiletics-based analyses of black preaching have given minimal at tention to the presence or absence of broad social issues and assumption reflected in black preaching. To some extent, sociological analyses have played a useful role in examining and understanding patterns within black preaching by adding some dimensions less explored through homiletics.

Analyses of black preaching and black worship by sociologists have largely focused on the socio-historical factors shaping black experience, and therefore the church's role, in the empowerment of blacks, not only spiritually, but also socio-politically. As early as the 1890s, Du Bois began identifying the contribution that preaching could make in the socio-political empowerment of blacks. Given this critical role, Du Bois urges that there is a great need for sermons to be a "regular source of real information," giving knowledge to the people to enable them to come into a fuller self-consciousness.

Similarly, sociologist E. Franklin Frazier, contends that because rac ism has denied blacks opportunities to realize their own human dignity, black worship and preaching have a vital role in "the affirmation and sup port of Black selfhood" and compensation for "the scars" from slavery and treatment as second class citizens .[18] For this reason, Frazier asserts that the role of the black church, "the invisible institution," "a nation within a nation," and "a refuge in a hostile white world," must be to enable blacks to give free expression to their deepest feelings, achieve a full sense of their human status, and experience their own existence as meaningful.

Assessing sermons by their ability to help black Christians experience the full sense of their human status and their existence as meaningful offers a useful measure often not employed in sermon analyses.

16. LaRue, *Heart of Black Preaching* 24.

17. Du Bois, "Negro Church," 86.

18. Mitchell, *Black Preaching*, 36.

19. Frazier, *Negro Church in America*, 44.

incoln and Mamiya focus their work on traditional approaches to the function of sermons. They emphasize that along with the role of glorifying God, sermons have served a range of functions throughout the historical development of the Black Church—namely, theological education, performative art, political advice, personal/social inspiration, moral formation, and therapy.[20] Lincoln and Mamiya note that while there are varying schools of thought among black preachers about the role of sermons, there remains a strong majority who suggest that preaching is about presenting the redemptive power of Jesus Christ, and not about debating social and political issues.[21]

Based on their sermon analyses, Lincoln and Mamiya make two critical observations. First, while the majority of black preachers have increased their articulation of racial concerns, race-consciousness, and race-affirmation in their sermons, "this should not obscure the fact that an evangelical gospel largely unconcerned with racial matters still has a strong [22] Second, Lincoln and Mamiya observe deep-seated, race-based inferiority reflected in the sermons of a majority of African American Lincoln and Mamiya's study also reflects the tendency of black religious scholars to engage in analyses of the black preaching tradition almost singularly focused on how black churches have become institutions that have helped blacks survive the racism in the U.S. Limited attention is given to broader social issues.

final thread of black religious hermeneutic is offered from the field of anthropology. Hans Baer adds an important perspective regarding the impact of black religious experience and preaching not clearly reflected in traditional homiletical or sociological approaches. Baer states, "Powerless groups have often utilized religion as a way of coping with social reality, and in this regard Black Americans are no exception."[24] Similar to Lincoln and Mamiya, Baer suggests that black religious movements have a "contradic- —on one hand, the role of religion has been used to compensate

incoln and Mamiya, *Black Church in the African American Experience*, 175.
s research is based on a study of more than 2,150 pastors of historically black churches across the U.S.

195.

176.


*Black Spiritual Movement*, 201.

160.

for what is not available to blacks in the wider U.S. context; the other role, however, has served to encourage blacks to embrace as their own goals the mainstream American values and goals, namely, individual achieve ment and material success. Focus on these goals and values, Baer argues, diminishes the likelihood of blacks engaging in critical reflection on the victimizing processes abounding in American society and often results in blacks blaming themselves and others for their inability to climb social and economic ladders.[26] Baer's analysis underscores the potential influences double-consciousness as it intersects with normative assumptions about power, race, gender, and class that are imbedded in sermonic language.

While traditional black religious hermeneutics analyze black preach ing relative to a focus on helping black Christians to deal with the anti-black racism, each of the following approaches facilitates a distinctive hermeneutical lens that will enable greater awareness of assumptions about social relations present in the normative language of sermons.

## Feminist-Womanist Hermeneutical Strategies

This study is not limited to a focus on gender in power relations in black churches, yet in looking at the various ways a power-*over* dynamic can be reflected in clergy-congregants relations, issues of gender and sexuality are central to any discussion of power. In addition to a critique of gender politics within churches, feminist-womanist analytical approaches bring an important focus to intra-group dynamics of justice that are essential to a comprehensive discussion of power.

Throughout the twentieth and into the twenty-first century, the criti cal inquiry about social relations reflected in religion, especially in the lan guage and practices of black churches brought by feminists and womanists continues to play a significant in helping the church live its mission more fully to be a resource of empowerment for all people. A womanist-feminist approach provides critical understandings needed to interrogate the spe cific elements of power that I have proposed in this study—namely, author ity, charisma, and trust. A womanist hermeneutic directly addresses issues of power relations in black church settings. A feminist critique fosters the use of analytical frameworks that extend beyond the traditional arena of black church culture, and thus, provides new lenses and strategies for un derstanding and discussing the black church.

26. Ibid.

Iris Marion Young offers two critical approaches useful for this analysis: critical normative theory and division of labor. Young argues that a key ingredient for developing a feminist critical theory of justice is to recognize that "the normative ideals used to criticize a society are rooted in experience of and reflection on that very society,"[27] and that these ideals emerge most clearly from listening to the voices of those who suffer in the societies. Young contends that the goal of critical normative theory is to utilize the echoes of suffering to guide the development of an "alternative vision of social relations" that provides the impetus for social change. The theory of justice emerges from a focus on the division of labor in workplaces, specifically how differences in gender, race, culture, education, and so on are understood and related to in ways that over-privilege some and under-privilege others. Young argues,

> hierarchical division of labor that separates task-defining and task-executing work enacts domination, and produces or reinforces at least three forms of oppression: exploitation, powerlessness, and cultural imperialism.[28]

ere, the third form of oppression that Young names "cultural imperialism" will be characterized as "ministerial imperialism."

Young's argument applies to what Patricia Hill Collins refers to as "the curriculum" which establishes and perpetuates hierarchical power relations. Young's division of labor theory can be used to characterize the relationship between black clergy (predominately males) and congregants, in which clergy define the parameters of the spiritual power and moral authority and define the issues deemed critical for congregants' lives, and where congregants are expected to execute their prescribed power and authority within the parameters as defined by their pastors. Young's argument is also consistent with Frazier's contention that during the early formation of black churches, black male clergy were authoritarians who "achieved a position of dominance" in the lives of congregants.[29]

Young's framework helps us to identify whether sermons foster "exploitation, powerlessness, and cultural imperialism" or promote the mission of the church to inspire and empower black Christians. This determination will be made by assessing whether the sermon texts reflect a

Young, *Justice and the Politics of Difference*, 5.

12.

Frazier, *Negro Church in America*, 17, citing Frederick Douglass, "the preacher was one of the slave notabilities." See Douglass, *Life and Times of Frederick Douglass*, 31.

use of ministerial authority to: (a) define the parameters of moral authority by which black Christians are expected to live their lives without question, or (b) contribute to the empowerment of churchgoers to use their own connections with God, interpretation of scripture, and lived experiences to share in defining the moral task of the church and for themselves.

The formation of churchwomen's associations in black Baptist and Methodist denominations in the early twentieth century is an example of how women were seeking to self-define and provide their own moral direc tion.[30] In her study of the formation of these associations, Higgenbotham posits that women's associations emerged as women were seeking to not only to demonstrate their respectability in response to racist characterizations of black women as overly sexualized and immoral, but also to eradicate the gender subordination of women that was preached in the black church.[31]

The emphasis of the womanist analysis on the role of sermons in the creation or perpetuation of liberative or oppressive values and practices in the black church is a key to ethically assessing sermons. One of the ways a womanist analysis provides a critical interpretive framework is through an exegetical focus on language.

Christian ethicist Katie Cannon explains that a womanist analysis "holds together the spiritual mix of black religious culture while exposing the complex, baffling contradictions inherent in androcentric language." womanist perspective does not ignore the richness of the black preaching tradition but enables a more comprehensive examination of the meaning and implications of the liberative-oppressive dichotomies in sermons and overall practices in the black church experience. Cannon constructs a womanist her meneutic of black preaching from the intersection of feminist liberationist

---

30. Early churchwomen brought their own analyses of black preachers and black preaching that has largely been overlooked by traditional black hermeneutics offered by black male religious scholars. For example, Nannie Helen Burroughs, one of the found ers of the Women's Auxiliary in the National Baptist Convention in 1900 categories of ministers: (1) the largest group were poorly educated, under-financed yet conscientious and well-meaning, (2) the second largest group were intellectually inept and exploited their congregations, and (3) the smallest and most respected group were well-trained theologians who sought to address contemporary social issues. Burroughs further asserted that women, representing the largest numbers of members and the larg est financial base of churches, had a right to well-trained clergy. Higgenbotham, *teous Discontent* ,176.

31. Ibid., 151ff.

32. Cannon, *Katie's Canon*, 114.

and black homiletical perspectives to re-envision overall power relations in the black church community. Cannon contends that black sermons must be examined with regard to "'how they participate in creating or sustaining oppressive or liberating socioethical values and sociopolitical practices.'"[33]

For Cannon, the primary purpose of black preaching is to inspire and call a worshiping community to "an ultimate response to God" in relation to a contemporary issue that the preacher addresses while proclaiming the Word of God. An ultimate response to God involves conscious action. Cannon argues that black preachers have a responsibility to present issues of justice to their congregations so that black churchgoers might make decisions for or against direct participation in emancipatory praxis. Therefore, an examination of preaching requires attention not only to "the nature of rhetorical strategies," but also to their "underlying ethics." Through its curriculum effect, preaching forms what we believe and why and facilitates the sacred moments in which creeds are reformed, social power is questioned, and traditions are transformed.[34]

To examine how sermons fulfill this function, a womanist critique investigates three distinct issues about sermon texts: (1) how meaning has been constructed, (2) whose primary interests are served, and (3) what kind of world is envisioned. Cannon contends that without exploring these queries the meanings and interpretations that preachers have "inherited" from their forebears, including systemic gender oppression that has been handed down in the preaching tradition, will play a major role in constructing the sermon.

Focusing on systemic gender oppression in black churches, Christian ethicist Marcia Riggs contends that both clergy and congregants reinterpret their beliefs about justice in order to reconcile those beliefs with systemic sexual-gender oppressive practices already in place.[35] Riggs argues that black churches commonly maintain that these interpretations are consistent with the Bible and church tradition. She provides a useful definition of "oppression" by which we can critique sermons,

> the processes by which relationships of imbalanced power between social groups is maintained, thus privileging one group

---

118.

iggs uses the term "sexual-gender" to reflect the relationships between men and women based on biological differences (sexual) and the socially constructed meanings of male and female (gender). Riggs, *Plenty Good Room*, 21.

over another and thereby limiting, injuring, and/or controlling the less privileged group.[36]

Given the ongoing reinterpretation of scripture and tradition to justify and normalize sexual-gender oppression in the black church, that in order to disrupt this pattern, a more evaluative framework for doing ethical reflection is needed. She proffers a womanist liberationist critique informed by the lived experiences of women in the black church as its ana lytical lens. This critique assists in identifying a pattern of reinterpreting scripture to justify intragroup dynamics of sexual-gender oppression, and thus, helps assess the degree of black preachers' complicity, accountability, and responsibility for reinforcing that oppression. Engaging the analysis of common teachings and practices within the black church with framework provides a prism for ethical reflection of black sermons that breaks through sexist justifications for hierarchal, oppressive power rela tions that exist in some black denominational churches. Such a womanist ethical reflection aids in the unveiling of oppressive relations often con cealed by institutional or group moral norms.

As Cannon posits, the meanings that are constructed through black preaching hinge upon what kind of world is envisioned, and whose interests and experiences guide that vision. In black churches, where high premium is extended to the authority and charisma of black male preachers, ministerial and denominational interests generally supersede the interests of congre gants. Thus, the present investigation of the black preaching tradition will be framed by Cannon's query about whether sermons participate either in creating and sustaining liberating values and practices, or oppressive ones.

This integration of womanist and feminist critical approaches helps us to explore what constitutes justice and oppression from two slightly differ ent, but not mutually exclusive, perspectives, thus enabling a more compre hensive examination of the implications of black preaching for black laity and clergy, men and women.

## Post-Critical Hermeneutics

Post-critical hermeneutics[37] looks more specifically at how the values and worldviews of speakers influence and are influenced by the tradi

36. Ibid., 104.

37. Physical chemist Michael Polyani is credited as one of the pioneers of post-critical

tions and social relationships. By exploring sermon texts to identify black preachers' values and worldviews, we gain an important analytic tool for assessing how issues of power reflected in sermons are also likely present in clergy-congregant relations within the church. Thus, post-critical hermeneutical methods assists us in exploring how the worldviews of preachers expressed through the black preaching tradition may unconsciously participate in creating or perpetuating liberative and/or oppressive beliefs and practices in the black church.

post-critical analytic method emphasizes how the interpretative and mediating role of preachers greatly shapes how congregants navigate how they live in society. Recognizing that this role is often engaged in unconsciously, post-critical hermeneutics urges that in order to understand the full meaning of the interpretive activity at work in sermons, we must simultaneously factor in the socio-historical context that shapes the ethical and moral foundations of the preachers.

Post-critical hermeneutics reflects an analytical approach that not only examines the historical and literary issues present in a text, but also emphasizes the specific contemporary context in which a sermon text is delivered. Clergy interpret scripture and tradition through their own worldviews, and therefore, post-critical hermeneutical methods can assist us in understanding the elements and implications of interpretive activity common to the black preaching tradition.

Distinct from homiletical approaches which commonly focus almost exclusively on the theo-sociological contexts which shape sermons, post-critical hermeneutics requires an examination of the liturgical contexts as well in order to understand the interpretive work occurring within the preacher and the church community. Because liturgical contexts reflect the social systems and structures that are distinctive to particular worshiping communities as well as the larger social context which frames the worship experience, post-critical methods assist in engaging comprehensive analyses that can lead to clearer understandings of the ethical implications that are present.

---

thought "relating critical thought to the precritical location within religion, tradition, culture and community, all of which critical thought had depreciated or discarded as unnecessary." McCoy, "Postcritical and Fiduciary Dimension in Polyani and Tillich," 6. In his discussion of theologian Paul Tillich's contribution to post-critical hermeneutical thought, McCoy contends, "Tillich moved beyond the pretensions and dichotomies that brought critical thought to an impasse and sought ways to combine the wholeness of human experiencing in the precritical era with the rigor and openness to liberation and innovation characterizing the critical era." Ibid., 8.

Liturgical studies scholar Lawrence Hoffman argues that the essential factor in examining social context

> is not geography at all, but the extent to which a community's mem bers identify themselves as sharers of a given situation, specific to themselves . . . From a shared sense of social distinctiveness, there arise the attitudes and aspirations that make for group identity.

Beginning with an appreciation for the cultural context facilitates an en gagement with the holistic network of interrelationships especially present in oral liturgical traditions. Oral liturgy must be socially-located in order to be fully comprehended. It is virtually impossible to understand the network of interrelationships in the oral liturgy without first studying the cultural import of its language, symbols, and rituals. As Saliers contends in *as Worship*, liturgical language is both shaped by and emerges from lan guage of cultural context. According to Saliers, "No study of liturgical texts can do without the study of the cultural patterns of communication and the character of social interaction that constitute these more 'tacit' dimensions of the celebrating assembly's life over a period of time."[39]

Homiletics scholar Fred Craddock emphasizes the most critical ben efit of contextualizing sermons is gaining a comprehensive understanding of the meaning of sermons for both preachers and hearers. Craddock offers four focal points to accomplish this contextualization process: ( *preaching tradition* of a particular pulpit, congregation and denomination, (2) *preacher-congregation* relationship, (3) *corporate culture* a gathered community, and (4) *theological* conversation that begins with the preacher's own beliefs, and then dialogues with the hearer's values, con victions, and experiences.[40] Two of Craddock's suggested foci—preacher-congregant relationships and corporate culture, in particular, point to the nexus between authority, charisma, and trust and the interpretive activity engaged in sermon-making.

Although not expressly identifying himself as a post-critical herme neut, the focus of black homiletics scholar James Harris on "the being of the preacher" is very post-critical. Harris contends that the "being of the preacher" is as integral to the sermon as the words themselves, and argues that sermons are reflections of a preacher's interpretations and worldview.

38. Hoffman, *Beyond the Text: A Holistic Approach to Liturgy*, 69.

39. Saliers, *Worship as Theology*, 153.

40. Craddock, *Preaching*, 32.

41. Harris' argument is based on the definition of preaching espoused by G.

Further, he posits that "everything about sermonic discourse is grounded in interpretation, and interpretation is grounded in understanding . . . Every sermon is an interpretation of a text but also its context and presuppositions or unwritten form."[42]

Post-critical hermeneutics play a vital role in helping us to demystify some aspects of preaching as a method for examining the intersection of social relations within congregations, cultural traditions and norms, preachers' individual worldviews and biographies, and the content and form of sermons. Post-critical hermeneutical method identifies the multivalent factors that influence black preaching (as well as preaching in other contexts), and as a result, de-centers the treatment of black preaching as if it were only "the inspired word of God." This de-centering is significant in that it enables us to break through the tendency to hold as sacred all or most of what is preached, without comprehensive critical examination of the preached word. Post-critical hermeneutics does not seek to dismiss or devalue the activity of divine inspiration in sermons, but rather seeks to acknowledge the wholeness of the sermonic experience—spiritual, religious, sociological, historical, economic, psychological, intellectual, and so on. This approach, thus, facilitates more comprehensive analysis of the content and form of black preaching—keeping the inspiration as sacred without regarding all that is preached as an untouchable, un-critique-able "sacred cow."

## Sociological Rhetorical Criticism

Distinctive from black religious, feminist-womanist, and post-critical hermeneutical methods, which are rooted in religious and liturgical studies fields, the fourth method, sociological rhetorical criticism, emerges from the field of speech criticism.[43] Because sociological rhetorical criticism focuses on speechmaking and rhetoric across genres and audiences, it offers

---

sermon is a statement of faith, drawn from the context of tradition, projecting the authentic being of the preacher." Harris, *Word Made Plain*, 38.

51ff.

ne of the early pioneers of rhetorical analysis, Lionel Crocker, sought to examine the patterns of speechmaking, and the speechmakers and their audiences. Crocker sought to assess the impact of several tools of rhetoric on effectiveness of speeches, as determined by audience responses. The tools Crocker outlined were: purpose of the speech, audience support for the theme (prior to the speech), the speaker's motivation, the speaker's identification with the audience, language form and style, and overall arrangement and organization of ideas. See Crocker, *Rhetorical Analysis of Speeches*.

fresh perspectives on black preaching that have not generally been available through the typical religiously-oriented analytic methods. By using theo logical hermeneutic as a starting point, religiously-oriented analytic methods may give less attention to critical socio-psychological, economic, and po litical issues expressed in sermons. These religion-rooted methods may tend treat these societal issues as part of the background to the theological when the inverse may be the case. For this reason, incorporating this method with the other three approaches fosters a more comprehensive examination of the sermon texts and their ethical implications. Again, it enables us to move be yond the treatment of all aspects of the preached word as sacred cows.

Because of the theological content of sermons, there is often a ten dency to regard them as distinctive from other genres of speech. While content across various genres of speech is unique, several key issues are present across genres, including sermons, such as, (1) the nexus of social context and speech content, and (2) the impact of societal structures, tradi tions, norms, and conventions upon both speechmakers and audiences.

Rhetorical critic Bernard Brock contends that the function of rhe torical criticism is to point out the particular "symbolic inducements" utilized in the speechmaking process to garner an audience's coopera tion.[44] What Brock refers to as "symbolic inducement" might more likely be framed as "inspiration" in traditional theologically and liturgically- oriented discussions of sermons as speech. The term "inducement," how ever, may at times be a more accurate reflection of the preaching process, where the preachers go beyond a goal to inspire and stir congregants to follow a particular path, but actively seek to instill particular beliefs in congregants in order to persuade, or induce them to behave in certain ways and make certain choices as defined by preachers.

The subtle distinction between inspiration and inducement is critical in recognizing the implications of all three elements of power— authority, charisma, and trust in the clergy-congregant relationship. *spiration* may be viewed as presenting a range of theoethical challenges and choices for congregants to make as rooted in their relationship with in God. Whereas *inducement* may be seen as a non-coercive or coercive

---

44. Brock, *Methods of Rhetorical Criticism: A Twentieth-Century Perspective* Brock defines *rhetoric* "as the human effort to induce cooperation through the use of symbols." Ibid., 14. *Criticism* is defined as "a reason-giving activity" that posits a par ticular judgment, explains the reasons for that judgment, and focuses on a specific social objective in effort to change an aspect of the human condition. Ibid., 12–13.

method for directing congregants' choice and their actions based on their relationship with or reliance upon the preacher.

Central to the sociological rhetorical criticism method is the tenet that all speech includes some texts that mediate power in one form or oth-ny query about the role of preaching, then, must examine the "power texts" within sermons and how those texts create or perpetuate particular beliefs and practices relating to assumptions about power, race, gender, and class. Investigation of power texts must also include a look at the contexts in which those texts are more likely used, by whom they are used, the socio-historical origin of their use, the nonverbal speech accompanying the texts, and the contemporary implications of those texts.[46]

The sociological critical perspective regards all human communication as both a productive force in society and as a reflection of society. Rhetori-nthony Hillbruner posits that speechmaking must be understood both as reflecting various social realities in a given context as well as directly contributing to those social realities.[47] Hillbruner emphasizes that the con-text which shapes the speaker "leaves an indelible stamp" upon the speaker which is then conveyed to the speaker's audience, a process which Hillbruner refers to as an "environmental determinism."[48] Environmental determinism, illbruner contends, reflects the ways in which the social realities and lived experiences of individuals influence the kinds of issues that these individuals address, as speakers, and the kinds of perspectives that they bring to those issues. In light of environmental determinism, black preaching reflects such realities as double-consciousness, ambiguous social ethic, ambiguous self-esteem, and more that are shaped by black experience in the U.S.

While I am not suggesting that all speech is determined exclusively by the social realities and lived experiences of individuals, recognizing the role of preachers' personal biographies in shaping the theological and social hermeneutics from which preachers sermonize is helpful for sermon analysis. That is, sermons both shape and are shaped by the so-cial context of structures and traditions, as well as the life experiences of preachers and audiences. The "indelible stamps" of life experiences are

433.

436.

277, quoting Hillbruner, "Speech Criticism and American Culture," 165.

277, quoting Hillbruner, "Rhetoric, Region, and Social Science," 174. While illbruner's "indelible stamp" theory, I urge readers not to regard his theory of "environmental determinism" as immutable.

imprinted upon the ways that preachers, as interpreters and interlocutors, transmit particular worldviews that have shaped them. Rhetorical critical method breaks through the presumption that all sermon content is solely a representation of scripture or "the word of God," and helps us recognize the interpretive activity present in sermons that is filtered through the lens of preachers' life experiences and beliefs.

The issues of power are present in all speech and function either rein force or detract from the messages about power imbedded in the prevail ing "national rhetoric," or meta-narrative.[49] A meta-narrative or national rhetoric is a master story developed and promoted by a dominant group that shapes the self-definitions, the ways of understanding and relating to the world, and parameters of power that are proscribed to everyone, across groups, who are a part of that larger culture.

An example of this is the meta-narrative that has prevailed as a na tional rhetoric in the U.S. since slavery, that blacks are inferior to whites. The internalization and perpetuation of this meta-narrative has greatly contributed to the inner warring, or double-consciousness, within the col lective psyche of black people. Another example of a meta-narrative is the theology of apostolic succession within the Christian church that contends that spiritual leaders receive their authority from God, and therefore, their authority is unparalleled within the church community and is not be ques tioned.[50] In this way, black preaching can be understood as either reinforc ing or subverting a national rhetoric within the U.S. of race, gender, class, and other forms of oppression.

Sociological rhetorical criticism explores the nonverbal, symbolic ac tion as part of the power of texts as well. Understanding nonverbal activity in this way invites us to investigate various sermonic devices as possible forms of sermons that reflect power relations. For example, the "call and response," a communal dialogic speechmaking style brought from West African culture, may be explored as an expression of the power relations in the black church as well as part of the participatory communal experience. Along with comments initiated by worshipers, such as "A plain," and "Preach," preachers often provide specific directives for how worshipers are to participate through words and actions. For example, "Say 'Amen,' church," and worshipers respond "Amen," or "You need to give God some praise right now," and in response, worshipers variously clap, lift their

---

49. Ibid., 281.

50. See chapter 1, "Holy Trinity," for a fuller discussion of apostolic succession.

hands and/or give other verbal expression of praise. The aspects of this participation that are not self-directed invite attention in our analysis of the sermons to assess the implications of the call-and-response tradition for the power relations between clergy and congregants.

## An Interdisciplinary Hermeneutical Approach

The traditional black religious hermeneutics play an important role in cataloguing the ways in which the black preaching tradition inspires and empowers black churchgoers to claim God's presence and power with them in the midst of anti-black racism. A feminist-womanist perspective provides the framework for exploring patterns of relating within the black church that are liberative and/or oppressive for the masses within the church. A post-critical hermeneutics approach aids us in expanding our understanding of traditional black preaching as an interpretive activity that indicates the vision of the world held by black preachers and how their visions greatly determine how churchgoers live in the larger society. And a sociological rhetorical criticism perspective guides us to acknowledge both sermons and symbolic action as mediating power in some form or another.

The integration of these sermon text criticism methods suggests that sermons are interpretive, persuasive arguments presented by preacher-mediators who reflect the socio-historical contexts, worldviews, aspirations, struggles, and fears of themselves and other black churchgoers. These methods also help us to acknowledge the long-term influence of the earlier generations of black preaching upon us today and the potential implications of what we preach today on future generations of black Christians.

This investigation provides an interdisciplinary hermeneutical approach that utilizes theoethical (black homiletics) understandings of the role of black preaching, explores whether norms within the black preaching tradition contribute to the perpetuation or dismantling of oppressive, disempowering messages and practices in the large public sphere (womanist-feminist critical theory), then examines how black sermons mediate messages about social power that are similar or dissimilar to messages prevalent in the larger society (sociological rhetorical criticism), and finally, factors in the influence of preachers in shaping congregants' worldviews about how to live in society (post-hermeneutical criticism).

Despite the potential of this integrated approach to provide rich hermeneutical insight, liturgical studies scholars Robin Leaver and Joyce Ann

Zimmerman contend that the full benefits of critical analyses can be lost as researchers tend to engage specific, narrow hermeneutical perspectives somewhat unconsciously. Therefore, in the interest of bringing maximum hermeneutical honesty and enhance the potential text analyses,
Zimmerman urge researchers to engage in self-reflection on the critical question: How do this researcher's hermeneutical perspectives shape the reading of or insights about the sermon and its contexts?[51]
hermeneutical perspective relating to black preaching tradition by sharing more of my biography as a template for the biographies of the preachers being examined here.

As a black woman preacher who grew up in the black Pentecostal church in the 1960s and 1970s, I learned a great deal about the intersection of race and class, growing up in a working class black neighborhood and be ing educated in predominately middle to upper-middle class white schools. My academic training included a bachelor's degree with a double major in psychology and sociology, and graduate degrees in law and theology. Prior to entering seminary and professional ministry, my professional experi ence included work as a manager, mediator, and organization development consultant in various business and community service sectors for almost twenty years. The combination of these diverse academic disciplines and professional work, along with my church experiences are reflected in my approach as a scholar and preacher to the ethics of power. My experiences in church and society fostered a lifelong interest in exploring the intersec tions of race, gender, class and other social factors used in power relations to assess similarities and differences in how these factors are treated in black churches relative to their treatment in the larger society.

Just as a researcher's life experience is reflected in her or his analyses, so also are the life experiences of preachers reflected in their sermons. For that reason, the analyses of the sermons by Bishops T. D. Jakes, Vashti McKenzie, and Eddie Long, will be framed by brief biographical informa tion to contextualize their respective theoethical beliefs about power rela tions and social justice as reflected in their sermons. Their biographical information will be used as tools for explicating the presence of possible environmental deterministic influences upon the preachers' worldviews, beliefs, and values expressed through their sermon content, that are then conveyed to their audiences.

51. Leaver, *Liturgy and Music*, 42.

# PART II

# The Righteousness of Christianity

As a social and business institution the church has had marvelous success and has done much for the Negro people, but it is needless to say that its many other activities have not increased the efficiency of its function as a teacher of morals and inspirer to the high ideals of Christianity . . . [W]e need . . . men who will really be active agents of social and moral reforms in their communities. There, and there only, is the soil which will transform the mysticism of Negro religion into the righteousness of Christianity.[1]

IN HIS 1898 MOREHOUSE College graduation speech Du Bois asserts that the critical role of black preachers must be to foster moral and social re-

Du Bois emphasizes that in order for the church to carry out this function ministers must actively preach and provide the quality of leadership that inspires black Christians to participate in bringing about needed social and moral reforms.

s Cleophus LaRue has argued, black preaching defines the message and mission of black churches. But what is the message about power conveyed through black preaching? What do sermons reflect about the

Du Bois, "College-Bred Negroes" in *Writings*, 837–38.

Many of these all male graduates were considering a career in ministry. Delores S. Williams points to the dualism within Du Bois as he address college graduates at Morehouse and Spelman Colleges, respectively. Even though Du Bois spoke about the need for black women's freedom, he also urged for black women to function within prescribed roles of "a civilized, progressive society," as he did in a speech to women graduates of Spelman College. See Williams, *Sisters in the Wilderness*, 214.

mission of black churches today? To what extent is the black pulpit used to inspire, empower, and equip black Christians to use their individual moral authority? How are sermons of today empowering black church goers to be Christians who are not merely as followers of the Christian tradition, but collaborators with God?

Peter Paris contends that, despite the common claim that black ser mons uplift and empower, black preaching fails to empower the human agency of black Christians. According to Paris, black sermons give their attention almost exclusively to a reliance on God's power, and ignore what black Christians can do themselves using their own personal and collec tive agency to bring about needed social changes.[3] Failure to emphasize the personal agency of black Christians limits the sense of freedom and inde pendence available through the black church experience to the confines of black church buildings and does not substantively foster the degree of em powerment needed to express this freedom in the broader, racist society. Although black churchgoers may experience a sense of emotional freedom while gathered together as a congregation, the emotionally freeing worship experience does not sufficiently equip them with a sense of empowerment that strengthens their individual ethical agency in society nor sufficiently challenge them to engage their moral authority for social justice activism.

While I agree with Paris' suggestion that black churchgoers are not being sufficiently empowered with regard to their ethical agency, there is a measure of empowerment that does occur in historically black denomina tions that is worth noting. Much of the focus, however, is on individual istically-oriented empowerment for psychological healing and economic prosperity, with only limited equipping black Christians to engage their ethical agency for social healing, justice, and transformation. The com mon sermonic themes and patterns of delivery have been transmitted from preacher to preacher through the long-term tradition of black preaching circuits. Cleophus LaRue contends,

> most blacks continue to learn to preach by observing then imi tating the styles of preachers they have come to admire. It . . . is on the 'church circuit'—local and national gatherings, and tele vision and tape ministries—that their favorite preachers teach them how to preach.[5]

3. Paris, *Social Teaching of the Black Churches*, 94–95.

4. Ibid., 95.

5. LaRue, *Power in the Pulpit*, 10.

Black preaching circuits are not only the vehicle by which preachers learn to emulate the preaching styles of their favorite preachers as LaRue contends, they are also the venues through which black preachers become inculcated with the perspectives, ideologies, and beliefs of those whom they admire. The elements of authority, charisma, and trust have the same quality of impact upon preachers studying under the tutelage of "big name," well-known preachers on "the church circuit." That is, the "student" preachers tend to extend great deference to their favorite preachers, who display the symbols of authority and charisma deemed worthy of trust—speaking at large conferences, leading megachurches, and producing television ministries with high viewership, and so on.

s such, the role model preachers transmit their specific perspectives about power and other theoethical issues not only directly to their own congregations and audience bases, but also indirectly to even wider audiences of black Christians through other preachers who emulate them,

Kenzie, Jakes, and Long. Investigating these widely-acclaimed preachers will help identify any particular patterns that are transmitted and emulated with regard to social power and moral authority.

To set the framework for examining these contemporary role model preachers, I lift up some critical insights about the role of black preaching from two preachers who have had tremendous influence in shaping the black preaching tradition, especially in the twentieth century—Dr. Gardner C. Taylor, "the Dean of Black Preachers" and Dr. James A. Forbes, Jr., "the Preachers' Preacher."

## The Dean of Black Preachers

With a preaching ministry that has spanned over seven decades, Dr. Gardner C. Taylor, heralded as the "Dean of Black Preachers," has influenced the preaching style and content of black and other preachers perhaps more than anyone.[6] As one of the leaders in the 1960s Civil Rights movement and one of the founders of the Progressive National Baptist

Taylor, born in 1919, served as the senior pastor of Concord Baptist Church in Brooklyn, New York from 1948–1990, during which time the church membership grew 14,000. He has received wide recognition for his preaching, across religious and racial groups, including being invited as the preacher for a weekly national broadcast on the NBC "National Radio Vesper Hours" (1958 to 1970), invited as the leader of inaugural prayer services for President Bill Clinton (1993 and 1997), and awarded the Presidential Medal of Freedom (2000).

Convention, Taylor is known for his social and political activism despite the widely held criticism in the black church that the pulpit was no place for politics. Taylor's sermons reflect a strong emphasis on the empower ment of the moral authority of black Christians.

Throughout the 1960s, Taylor's sermons shifted to a greater urgency for justice and more strongly held people accountable for the work of jus tice. As he did, he simultaneously urged his hearers to be co-workers with God and emphasized personal responsibility for one's own actions. spoke beyond the normative parameters of the black preaching tradition which perceived racism as distinctive from other social ills, and proclaimed that the root of racism and other social ills was spiritual. H ambiguously promote liberative socioethical values and practices.

> Nothing is more tragic about the long season of injustice in this country than what it has done to so many young people and to their hopes and aspirations . . . The sense of God helps us not to think of ourselves more highly than we ought to, for in our aware ness of him as source of life we become sensitive to our creatureli ness, to the fact that we are neither source nor center of life . . . This weird disease of self-centeredness creates the foundation for racism, turns our family relationships into tense struggles for at tention and priority, prostitutes friendship into a tool for the satis faction of our own warped egos.[7]

Greatly informed by more than twenty years of involvement in civil rights activism and social reform, in his book, *How Shall They Preach?* Taylor explains his philosophy about preaching.

> The power and pathos of the preacher are to be found not in vol ume of voice nor those patently contrived tremors of tone preachers sometime affect, but in passionate avowals which . . . have gotten out of the written word into the preacher's own heart, have been filtered and colored by the preacher's own experiences of joy and sorrow, and then pressed upon the hearts and minds of those who hear.

While social justice activism is at the forefront of Taylor's preaching, what guides his understanding of the purpose of preaching is rooted in his conviction that Christians are called to be ambassadors of God. In his

7. Taylor, "A Total Answer" (November 6, 1969) in *Words of Gardner Taylor: NBC Radio Sermons*, 74.

8. McMickle, *Encyclopedia of African American Christian Heritage*

response to an interview question posed by Cleophus LaRue, "To what end do we preach?" Taylor proclaims,

> We are ambassadors of God's kingdom and we address the terms and ultimatums of that kingdom. Ultimate authority belongs to our king. Now I think we can get presumptuous at this, and I think one ought to try to do this with fear and trembling, because it is an awesome kind of idea.[9]

ooted in their personal connection with Jesus, Taylor's sermons urge, Christians—ordained and lay—to receive the authority needed for how they engage in the world.

> Black people have endured a great many things . . . The most sinister visitation of pain that we have known occurred in the long record of the attempt to push us out of the human family, to deny us our standing as human beings, to caricature how we looked. The old long idea that ran through so much of our pain in this country had to do with the image. Of course the image was done on the part of the oppressor trying to salvage its humanity by denying the oppressed its humanity aimed at denuding us of our dignity, stripping us of our participation in the human family . . . We are the descendants of those who would not be denied their humanity . . . Deeper than the ridicule was the outrage . . . visited upon our ord Jesus . . . In His own clothes.[10]

Taylor in a personal interview with Cleophus LaRue. LaRue, Power in the Pulpit, 146.

Taylor, "His Own Clothes" (Hampton Minister's Conference, 1982) *Essential Taylor* audiotape. The remainder of this sermon is a singular celebration of Jesus. Taylor neither comes back to nor links the effectiveness of Jesus in wearing "his own clothes" or to the moral strength of the ancestors "who would not be denied their dignity" to outline what is possible in the life of blacks in claiming their own spiritual and moral authority. As discussed in chapter 1, Lincoln and Mamiya found a race-based sense of inferiority reflected in the sermons of a majority of the black male preachers in their study. Lincoln and *Black Church in the African American Experience*, 176. Given this finding, to me it is questionable to what extent a transformative appropriation of the spiritual authority of Jesus Christ and a moral authority of black ancestors is really made more possible through the common rhythmic cadences of black preaching and to what extent black audiences are helped to reach beyond the realm of emotional titillation into the depths of the psychic injuries of racial oppression in order for the wounds of their souls to be healed. In this sermon, Taylor's affirmation of the spiritual and moral authority of preachers overlooks the sense of inferiority among black preachers that Lincoln and Mamiya observe. As McWhorter argues, "centuries of abuse left the race with an inevitable inferiority complex, well documented by black academics and psychologists." McWhorter, "Double Consciousness merica," 14. This sense of inferiority despite ongoing affirmation and preferential treatment extended to black male preachers signals the presence of Du Bois' theory of

Taylor emphasizes God's promise to participate in the efforts for jus tice, and that faith in God's promises is critical to winning the battle for justice. Taylor fosters the empowerment of black churchgoers by focusing on the spiritual power they have to overcome the challenges of the world as they trust in God.

In an interview conducted by Lincoln and Mamiya, Taylor acknowl edges the impact of the civil rights movement on his preaching content. Lincoln and Mamiya contend that in the 1960s Taylor's preaching began to include issues of racial concern, while also highlighting some of the futile aspects of the civil rights movement, such as the black liberation platform. As a result of the raising of his own black consciousness, Taylor's preaching began even more to empower and challenge his hearers to work for racial and other forms of social justice.

> You and I must not flee or sidestep the responsibility of trying to make this world a little more like God would have it. Jesus did not say to his people to flee from the earth's affairs but said rather, 'Go ye into all the world,' He would have changed to his will all of the world, business, politics, pleasure, every area of life . . . Thank God that there is an interior wealth of spiritual power and authority which is your birthright and by which you can determine your circumstance.[11]

During the late 1950s to early 1970s, there were major shifts in social realities in the U.S. impacting the lives of black and other significant ways, including, the Brown v. Board of Education Court decision[12] and development of black nationalism.[13] The presence of these and other developments signaled and fostered considerable ideologi cal shifts in the black culture and overall U.S. culture that may have con tributed to the shift in Taylor's preaching. During this era, Taylor began

double-consciousness present, but not examined, in the black preaching tradition.

11. Taylor, "Invisible Supplies" (delivered October 19, 1969) in *Taylor: NBC Radio Sermons*, 64–65..

12. The 1954 United States Supreme Court decision in *Oliver L. Brown et.al. v. the Board of Education of Topeka (KS) et.al.* marked a significant judicial turning point in the U.S. history, dismantling "the legal basis for racial segregation in schools and other public facilities." *Oliver L. Brown*, Brown Foundation.

13. A secular movement that placed an emphasis on the agency and ability of black Americans to work for the change that they longed for in the society, and no longer wait for deliverance by any force external to themselves, including the divine.

placing greater emphasis on human efficacy more central than in some earlier sermons, not instead of God's power but in collaboration with God.

> 'They shall walk, and not faint.' Here is the promise that along the hard, dusty road, when loads grow heavy and there's a dull sameness to every scene, power can belong to us not to give up, not to faint . . . So much of our trudging is in 'the light of common day,' where there is weariness, sweat, and hopes long deferred and youthful dreams that turned to dust in our hands. There is no more relevant promise God has made than this word . . . 'They shall walk, and not faint.' The condition of the gift of the promise is a willingness to wait on the tides of God to bear us up and on our brave and glorious voyages.[14]
>
> Someone young of years and hard of heart immediately cries out, 'This is exactly what I do not like about all this babbling of religion. I want to be doing things, not waiting.' . . . 'We have waited too long already,' some say. Ah, and thinking that is to miss the point. The kind of expectant waiting . . . is not the idleness of expecting our dreams to fall full-grown from the skies . . . No, rather it is meant that we are confident, while toiling, that God will strengthen and hold when our arms grow weary and our footsteps are labored and slow.[15]

Beginning in the late 1960s, Taylor spoke more directly to black and non-black Christians about their responsibility to participate with God in making "a world more like God would have it." Unlike most black ministers during this era who not even did address the issue of racism in America in all-black contexts,[16] Taylor boldly and prophetically addressed the "perennial problem of race" in his nationally syndicated weekly radio program listened to by racially diverse audiences.

> ur inability to make ourselves understood to one another can be illustrated in our long and shameful failure to establish a healing and purposeful dialogue in America's perennial problem of race . . . Christians cannot abandon this world and its needs. We must work for physical changes. This is the ancient tension of the people of God. This is a dying world, and yet God's people must speak to it the word of life . . . There is a power which is available

Taylor, "The Promise of Renewal" (delivered September 6, 1959) in *Words of Gardner Taylor: NBC Radio Sermons*, 43–44.

45.

incoln and Mamiya, *Black Church in the African American Experience*, 195.

> to us which we can have if we will . . . This is available to you. Appropriate it now. It is yours![17]

While Taylor proclaims the human condition as he perceives it, and urges his audience to speak "the word of life" to the world, he does not define for his audience what constitutes a word of life nor does he establish where, when, and how they should execute or speak that word.

Taylor leaves it to his audience to define the life-giving word for themselves, and thus, to use their own individual and collective power to "work for physical changes" needed in the society.

Taylor is one of few preachers who addresses the issue of social account ability. Unlike conventional focus on institutional appointment, apostolic succession, or charisma as the source of authority, Taylor contends that au thority comes through the courage to deal with the hardships and personal pains that come with life. His formula for authority makes no hierarchal distinctions or exclusionary claims that some individuals or institutions have the power to extend authority to others. As such, Taylor seeks to disrupt the forms of oppression that Iris Marion Young outlined as exploitation of those who are expected to execute the tasks defined by others, sense of powerless ness fostered in the minds of the task-executers, and cultural imperialism by those who define the task and direct others to adherence.

> There is in us this desire, this yearning to be effective, to have au thority, to have authenticity . . . How does one come to authority and power?' . . . So that somewhere in the wounds of the hands also resided the power to open the book . . . You and I will not want to court being hurt so we stay out of things in which we ought to be involved. We move along on the fringes of life's busy and urgent matters because we want to protect ourselves. But . . . any authenticity that we are going to have as persons of faith and any authority that we are going to have as witnesses to the gospel of Je sus Christ will come because of our exposure to bruises and scars. There is no other way to authenticity . . . an entrance into the full, the true authority, into the glorious liberty of the sons of God.

17. Taylor, "Invisible Supplies" (October 19, 1969) *Words of Gardner Taylor: NBC Radio Sermons,* 64–65. Emphasis added.

18. This text speaks to the issue of social power relations characterized by Iron Mar ion Young as "task-defining" and "task-executing" roles.

19. Taylor, "A Personal Word at Evening for Ministers and Others" (February at Trinity Lutheran Theological Seminary), *Words of Gardner Taylor: mons,* 161–62. In a footnote, Taylor writes, "This sermon is not from the National

Taylor reflects an instruction that is common in much of black preach-
*using* the harsh realities of racism and other challenges of life
that blacks have endured for their spiritual benefit. Taylor uses the suffering
motif, not merely to engender hope for individual Christian lives, but also
as a basis for visioning a more just society.

> Perhaps in thinking about our hurts, we attach too much impor-
> tance to what happens to us rather than looking at the results . . . For
> what is really grievous is not what happens but how it affects us . . .
> Jesus says, 'In the world you shall have tribulation, be of good cheer'
> . . . The Lord has worked on us that way because the Lord is not out
> to make us comfortable, but to make us conformable to his death
> and to his suffering . . . It takes some sighing and crying, hurting
> and bruises, pain and anguish, and anxiety and trouble and rain and
> winter and dark nights and high hills and lowly ways so that our
> prayer can be 'Have Thine own way, Lord . . . Thou are the potter I
> am the clay' . . . God is growing us into his likeness . . . Sorrow taught
> me to sing. Trouble taught me to pray . . . More power, do you want
> that? God doesn't have but one way to give that.[20]

major theme running through Taylor's sermons is that full spiritual authority and power only come through hardship and heartache. In
his critique of a growing emphasis in black preaching on financial prosperity, he states,

> Those of us who love the church and the gospel and the role of
> the preacher see so much that is discouraging. So many of our
> churches have become little more than social clubs or places for
> purposeless emotional orgy. Too many of us who preach seem to
> have little else in mind except . . . our own comfort and luxury.[21]

Taylor prophetically calls for Christians to use their spiritual power
and moral authority to participate in bringing forth justice and liberation,
not only for blacks, but the broader U.S. society. His examinations are clear
about the adverse impact of oppression upon the full humanity of both
those who are oppressed as well as those who are the oppressors. To foster
the co-creation of a society that recognizes and nurtures the full humanity
and gifts of all people, Taylor models a type of black preaching that expands

Pulpit, but is my legacy to those who come after me." Ibid., 159.

Taylor, "Seeing Our Hurts with God's Eyes" (Hampton Minister's Conference,
*Essential Taylor.*

Taylor, "Look Up!" in LaRue, *Power in the Pulpit*, 157.

the notions of authority beyond the prevailing exclusionary, hierarchical rhetoric in the U.S. society. This communal approach to authority lays a critical foundation for cultivating a sense of individual human agency within audiences to participate in a liberative and just vision of society.

## The Preachers' Preacher

Rev. Dr. James A. Forbes, Jr. is the Senior Minister Emeritus of The side Church in New York City, where he had served as the first black Senior Minster to lead this multicultural congregation from 1990 to serving at Riverside, Dr. Forbes was the first Joe R. Engle professor of preaching at Union Theological Seminary from 1976–1989, and now serves there as the Harry Emerson Fosdick Professor. Because of his considerable effectiveness as both a preacher and a teacher of preachers, in was voted one of the "12 Most Effective Preachers" in the English-speaking world.[22] Hailed as one of the nation's foremost preachers of the late twenti eth century, and widely known as the "Preachers' Preacher," as a rich resource for explicating the role of preaching and understanding the implications of what we preach.

Forbes is greatly shaped by being raised and formed in a black Pen tecostal denomination, The United Holy Church of America, and his later exposure and calling to the ecumenical church. In his book, and Preaching, he reflects on his journey into the preaching ministry,

> I have been a student of preaching most of my life. According to family lore, as a preschool lad I used to stand on a coffee table to imitate my father's fiery preaching style ... My grandfather, grand mother, several uncles and an aunt, and of course my father all were preachers ... After many years of resisting the call to become a preacher, I finally accepted the vocation.[24]

22. Baylor University worldwide survey of 341 seminary professors and editors of religious periodicals.

23. In national and international religious circles, The Rev. Dr. James known as the preacher's preacher because of his extensive preaching career and his char ismatic style. Based on the 1995 Baylor University Survey, *Newsweek* 4, 1996 issue recognized Forbes as one of the twelve "most effective preachers" in the English-speaking world.

24. Forbes, *Holy Spirit and Preaching*, 14.

Forbes notes the voracious appetite he developed to listen to, study, and learn from notable black preachers of the mid-twentieth century, including Mordecai Johnson, Howard Thurman, Samuel Proctor, Gardner C. Taylor, and Martin Luther King, Jr. At the same time, Forbes was also exposed to the teaching and writings of Christian theologians at Union Theological Seminary including Paul Tillich. Through these various experiences, Forbes developed a strong sense of God's calling to "progressive Pentecostalism," reflecting both an emphasis on the Spirit and a deep commitment to transformative social action.[25]

Forbes defines the preacher as

> a member of the community of faith who has been called, anointed, and appointed by the Holy Spirit to be an agent of divine communication . . . [and whose] authority is grounded in the self-revealing will of God . . . [and] confirmed or ordained by the community of faith.[26]

Forbes' identification of the preacher first as a member of the community is critical. The preacher is not to be elevated, high and lifted up, nor to be regarded as separate and distinctive, but rather one of the community members who has a specific anointing, role and responsibility in the community. For Forbes, given the import of the preacher's role and responsibility in the community, preaching that is grounded in anointing alone is not sufficient; preaching must also be rooted and strengthened by an ongoing openness to learn through study, coaching, and critique.

> Professionals who teach others need to be taught themselves. It is easy to fall prey to the notion that one has found the final form of excellence . . . It is most certainly the case with preaching where freshness of approach is sustained by the constant quest for the "more excellent way."[27]

s the challenges of the society shift and change and as the demands and conflicts in the lives of black churchgoers are different, and perhaps even more complex that yester-year, black preachers must be open to a "freshness of approach" not only with regard to preaching style but also preaching content. What is the fresh word from the Lord that black Christians need to hear today that help them live more fully equipped to

15.

19–20.

67.

appropriate the power of God in all aspects of their lives? What must contemporary preaching facilitate in the lives of black churchgoers today?

In an interview that I conducted with Forbes,[28] he argues that the primary purposes of contemporary black preaching are

> To preach prophetically, following the model of Jesus, who has given us a vision of justice, hope, peace, and love that extends to all people. The world needs the fruit of that vision and our lives cry out for it. Yet we are caught up in a social context that needs spiritual experience to empower us to impact the world. We must be engaged in a serious critique of the culture in order to live according to the Gospel, and look out for the needs of the community with a global vision.[29]

Forbes also urges that black preaching must empower and urge Americans to impact and transform the world as co-laborers with God. Much like Taylor, the Civil Rights Era was very important in shaping Forbes' theology of preaching.

> Martin Luther King introduced a new era in which preaching to save souls is no longer enough. The Civil Rights movement broadened the "salvation agenda." In light of this expanded agenda, God no longer is simply the one who cares for the saints; now the saints are called to care for others relating to the circumstances of their lives, not just their souls.[30]

Forbes, like Taylor, emphasizes a theology that focuses not only on what God can do for us but also reflects what we can do as collaborators with God and on behalf of God for others. For Forbes, the civil rights movement helped African American Christians broaden their sense of responsibility as co-workers with God for the care of the total human experience, not just the spiritual aspect of people's lives.

> We must be engaged in reshaping of the consciousness of many blacks. By and large, black churches are not engaged in this work. Having endured much hardship, terrorism, and oppression, blacks have a message from our own experience about the difference that the power of God can make. We must share the hope of that message to others, near and far. Our preaching must not only be for

---

28. Forbes, interview by Cari Jackson, January 22, 2002.

29. Ibid.

30. Ibid.

black communities, but for the world, helping all peoples move from victimhood to victorhood.[31]

In his book, *Whose Gospel: A Concise Guide to Progressive Protestant-*, Forbes invites all Christians to partner with God and with other people of faith in "addressing the serious problems facing our nation" as part of our calling from God.[32]

ccording to Forbes there were three major social factors, in concert with the Civil Rights movement, that play vital roles in shaping a new black consciousness,

> First, *urbanization*. As blacks have become more urbanized, the church no longer knows or is involved with your whole life. Thus, the church is no longer the sole arbiter of social values now that other options are available. As a consequence, secular elements are absorbed more into the church, resulting in a shift in theology. There is a reduction in confidence and reliance on the Holy Spirit. God has receded in the consciousness of people in these advanced stages of secularization. The church is impacted by this more than it knows. The availability of diverse resources for success and pleasure has impacted the frequency of turning to God.
>
> Second, the triumph of "mammon," *capitalism*. Blacks within the church and beyond it bounds, have been led to believe that acquiring materials brings happiness and a sense of worthiness. The broader culture distorts what real happiness and joy look like.
>
> Third, the *demonic use of emotionalism*. Many churches have led people to focus on "shouting" and "getting happy" as almost exclusive manifestations of liberation. After a good time of dancing and praising, the saints then leave church believing that they are liberated. This is pre-mature ejaculation. The work of liberation is not finished.[33]

To a great extent, after the desegregation of public schools, public transportation, and lunch counters, after the repeal of Jim Crow laws, after voting rights laws were passed, and after public lynchings have ceased to be a major form of killing blacks, much of black preaching stopped lifting up the continued need for "the work of liberation" for all people. Understanding that the process of liberation is always an ongoing enterprise, insights from both Taylor and Forbes provide a clarion call to black preachers to

Forbes, *Whose Gospel*, Loc. 87 (Kindle edition).

Forbes, interview by Cari Jackson, January 22, 2002.

urge and empower black churchgoers to engage in the work of liberation that is needed for the twenty-first century.

## The Continued Work of Liberation

Is there a word from the Lord that will heal, uplift, challenge, and empower black Christians today?

The following chapters present analyses of sermon texts from Bishops T. D. Jakes, Vashti Murphy McKenzie, and Eddie L. Long as examples of the kinds of messages that are being preached and that serve as models for other preachers. Because of their wide acclaim, each of these preachers has great influence upon both the preaching style and content of "sons" and "daughters" in the ministry. Through television broadcasts, social media networks, and "the church circuit," each of these preachers has significant influence upon the black preaching tradition that is being handed down today.

Although these preachers are most known for specific areas of focus in their respective ministries — Jakes (psychological and economic empowerment), McKenzie (leadership and social empowerment), and (economic and men's empowerment)—the sermons selected are designed to represent a cross-section of their sermon topics. None of the sermons presented were selected because of any overt sermon titles or themes about social power. The sermons included in this study were selected among those that: (1) were identified and marketed by the preachers as some of their premiere sermons, (2) collectively they span across the years during which the preachers were most well-known, and (3) were preached to diverse audiences, where possible. Choosing the sermons that the preachers have featured in their sermon portfolios may suggest the kinds of messages they regard as important for black Christians and others to receive. The excerpts of sermons discussed in the following chapters will be used to explore what themes about social power are conveyed and the implications of those themes for fostering or impeding the social liberation of black churchgoers in this century.

Using an interdisciplinary critical method, the sermon analyses are guided by three questions:

1. What explicit and implicit messages about social power relations are conveyed in the sermons, especially relating to clergy-congregant relationships, and how?

In what ways are the messages conveyed consistent with the prophetic purposes of black preaching to inspire a global vision of justice, hope, peace and love for all people, to critique the injustices within society, and empower black Christians to be co-laborers with God towards that vision?

ow do these messages help create/sustain socioethical values and sociopolitical practices that are oppressive or liberating?

## Paradigms of Preacher Power

ur investigation of the sermon texts of Jakes, McKenzie, and Long points to distinctive patterns relating to how sermons convey specific messages about authority, charisma, and trust. These sermonic patterns are illustrative of three approaches, or sub-traditions, within the black preaching tradition relating to social power. Namely,

*Economy of Power* (T. D. Jakes)—A priestly call primarily to black Christians to discern their individual divine destiny and to live in alignment with the authority of God for success in all areas of their lives; and

*Power to the People* (Vashti McKenzie)—A prophetic call to black Christians and others empowering them to use their individual and collective authority as co-laborers with God to heal and transform their own lives and the world;

*Under Submission* (Eddie Long)—A priestly call exclusively to black Christians inspiring them to access the power of God available to individuals as they follow the leadership of the priest-preacher.

These approaches are not intended to categorize all aspects of McKenzie, Jakes, and Long's preaching. These categorizations relate specifically to the kinds of messages they convey about social power relations, and especially, the moral agency of black Christians. Additionally, these approaches are not related to preaching style—rhetorical cadence, phrasing, and organization—rather they are ideological[34] in nature. That is, the preaching

The use of the term "ideologies" is informed by Karl Marx's definition of ideology as an instrument of social production, as set of doctrines or beliefs that form the basis of a political, economic or other system. Ideology itself represents the "production of ideas, of conceptions, of consciousness," all that "men say, imagine, conceive," and include such things as "politics, laws, morality, religion, metaphysics, etc." See Marx, *German Ideology with Selections from Parts Two and Three*, 47.

approaches highlight the distinctive worldviews of the preachers, especially relating to the nexus of their constructs of theology, economics, politics, and social ethics reflecting their messages about social power and moral authority. Distinguishing the specifics of these constructs aids us in recognizing the black preaching tradition as more than a monolithic style and theology of preaching. It also assists us in understanding the breadth of implications that black preaching has in the lives of black churchgoers.

# Economy of Power

In the long run, force defeats itself. It is only the consensus of the intelligent men [and women] of good will in a community or in a state that really can carry out a great program with absolute and ultimate authority. And by the same token, without the authority of the state, without force of police and army, a group of people who can attain such consensus is able to do anything to which the group agrees.[1]

CHARISMATIC GIFTS ARE VERY important indicators of spiritual authority in all aspects of black preaching. In the Economy of Power paradigm, charisma is of even more particular value. While preachers may be conferred their authority by church institutions, their authority is not dependent upon institutional channels. Preachers' authority is deeply rooted in their charismatic gifts to tap into and articulate the hurts and longings in people's lives and to provide simplistic spiritually-based formulas and solutions for an enhanced quality of life.

Charisma, regarded as a demonstration of spiritual authority from God and the primary resource for spiritual growth and abundance, is incontrovertibly bound to adherence to the words of the preacher. The preacher's life as a model for what is possible is another primary source for the ministerial
s McMickle contends, the preacher's charismatically-derived success is one of the sources and demonstrations of his authority.[2]

Du Bois, "Dusk of Dawn" in *Du Bois Writings*, 715.
McMickle, *Where Have All the Prophets Gone?*, 112–13.

Foundational to the Economy of Power approach is a worldview akin to the principle of manifest destiny[3] that highlight's the sovereignty of God, who assigns talents, gifts, and responsibilities to people who are ready to appropriate what God makes available for their lives. The distinctive char acteristics of this approach include: 1) highlighting the mistakes, hurts, hardships, and sins in people's lives and linking them with a presentation of God's divine purpose, 2) presenting God as one who bestows ability and authority in varying degrees to certain individuals, and 3) empowering in dividuals with strategies to transform their individual lives.

In addition to facilitating emotional release by providing worship environments in which black churchgoers are allowed and even encour aged to cry, dance, and sing, common in most models of black preaching, sermons in the Economy of Power paradigm address specific life struggles traditionally not spoken in black preaching. Preaching within the of Power paradigm is designed to help worshipers to identify specific life wounds and then provide healing strategies for addressing them. result of this open acknowledgement of painful life experiences historically silenced in black church culture,[4] this preaching model fosters a height ened degree of trust in and allegiance to the preacher who demonstrates the compassion to recognize and care enough about those specific pains and bring them to God on behalf of the individual and collective worshipers.

The Economy of Power approach generally does not address the pres ence of various forms of social oppression—race, gender, economic, etc. Nor do sermons in this approach urge black worshipers to participate in collective efforts for social justice. Instead, the general strategy for resolving these issues is to provide tools for black Christians to move themselves out of the harmful reach of these systemic oppressions by aligning themselves with the favor and abundance of God.

With its emphasis more focused on individual empowerment, of Power departs significantly from the purposes of black preaching outlined

---

3. According to Reginald Horsman, the theory of manifest destiny emerged from the "Enlightenment idea of progress [which] gave a whole new impetus to the image of America as an arena for the betterment of mankind." Horsman argues that running through the fabric of American culture is the idea that human progress is interconnected with American expansionism, and that this expansionism is a part of on behalf of humankind. See Horsman, *Race and Manifest Destiny*, 84.

4. See, for example, our earlier discussion in chapter one about clergy sexual miscon duct, describing how individuals who have been violated by clergy are often silenced and treated as the seducers and perpetrators. This pattern is consistent with the approach to sexual abuse within families often leaving individuals no safe space to be validated in and helped to heal from their experiences.

by Du Bois to teach morals needed for social reforms in black communities and Forbes to lift up a vision of justice for all people and equip black Christians to work as co-laborers with God toward the realization of that vision.

## Thomas Dexter Jakes

Bishop T. D. Jakes pioneered a new trend in the black preaching tradition that focuses on healing personal emotional wounds of black Christians, especially of women. Jakes has moved beyond the traditional function of black preaching to provide momentary generalized catharsis to using sermons to directly address a specific range of wounding life experiences that impact the lives of many black and other women. By highlighting the hurts, fears, and failings in individuals' lives, Jakes effectively points his audiences to the authority of God as a corrective resource for every aspect of their lives.

Born Thomas Dexter Jakes in West Virginia in 1957, Bishop T. D. Jakes has become one of America's premier entrepreneur-preachers. Jakes was the son of a schoolteacher mother and a father who owned a janitorial business. is father's protracted illness and subsequent death, during Jakes' childhood, resulted in a significant change to the family's financial condition going from middle class to working poor. Jakes majored in Psychology at West Virginia niversity, but was not able to complete college for financial reasons. He grew up worshiping in both Baptist and Pentecostal churches, and early on began using his musical gifts to earn income as a church musician.

1980, at the age of twenty-three, Jakes started a Pentecostal Ap- church with ten members, while working various industrial labor jobs to support his family. Expanding his ministry in 1990, Jakes moved from small town Montgomery, West Virginia to Charleston. Focused on continued expansion, Jakes moved his ministry to Dallas, Texas in . When Jakes moved this ministry, fifty families from his church in

Jakes is a bishop in Higher Ground Always Abounding Assemblies (founded by Bishop Sherman Watkins in 1988). Apostolics are a non-Trinitarian branch of Pentecostalism with a theology that emphasizes the oneness of God manifested in Jesus Christ.

*T. D. Jakes*, 21–22. See for example, excerpts from the Pentecostal Apostolic statement of faith of Transformation Church in, Baltimore, Maryland (Bishop Monroe Saunders, Jr., senior pastor): "We believe that the Bible is the word of God written by inspired men and that it is profitable for instruction in righteousness We believe in water baptism by full immersion; that baptism is done in the name and authority of Jesus Christ We believe in the baptism of the Holy Spirit with the attendant manifestation of speaking in tongues We believe that those who reject the gospel of Jesus Christ will be im on the last day." "Welcome to Transformation Church" website.

Charleston moved with him to Dallas. Jakes' church, the Potter's now has 30,000 members. Because of the tremendous national impact of Jakes' ministry, in 2001, *Time* magazine featured Jakes on the cover framed by the question, "Is This Man the Next Billy Graham?" The article marked the first time a black preacher was considered in the running to be America's "next leading religious luminary."[6]

In his biography on Jakes, sociologist Shayne Lee contends,

> In today's religious climate, many pastors run their churches like Fortune 500 corporations vying for market share. Like large con glomerates that make Americans passive victims of ads for pop drinks and sports cars, celebrity preachers use the airways, print media, and cyberspace to inundate Christian consumers with ads for sermon videos, music CDs, and conferences . . . No other min ister depicts our postmodern age of commercialized spirituality more than Bishop T. D. Jakes.[7]

Lee argues that Jakes' church, Potter's House, symbolizes an emerging new congregational model, the "new black church." Lee contends that Jakes has distinguished himself by combining

> otherworldly experience of ecstatic worship and spiritual enlight enment with a this-worldly emphasis on style, image, and eco nomic prosperity . . . and willingness to contextualize Christianity for contemporary needs and culture, while not compromising a vigorous support for biblical authority.[8]

Jakes has entered into prominence as a neo-Pentecostal era of postdenominational Protestantism,[10] both shaping and being shaped by a change in the religious landscape. Expanding beyond the therapeutic expression of traditional black worship, the sermons of Jakes and other

6. Lee, *T. D. Jakes*, 21.

7. Ibid., vii.

8. Ibid., 5.

9. Neo-Pentecostalism is a spiritual movement that began emerging in the among non-Pentecostal black churches, especially African Methodist and various Baptist conventions. Characteristics of neo-Pentecostalism include less for mal, highly spirited worship services, deep spiritual piety, and progressive political activ ism. See Lincoln and Mamiya, *Black Church in the African American Experience*

10. Donald Miller argues that post-denominationalism, a new paradigm for can Christianity is a "second Protestant reformation." According to Miller, there are hundreds of "new-paradigm churches" creating new genres of worship and greater democratization of sacred ritual, and a postmodern medium of presentation. Miller, "Postdenominational Christianity in the Twenty-First Century," 197.

preachers of the new black church are themselves therapeutic messages. Jakes has successfully cultivated books, conferences, and television preaching ministry into a business brand that centers on the themes of healing from emotional brokenness and on economic empowerment.

ee describes Jakes as characteristic of "a postmodernist preacher" who

> saturates the marketplace with an incessant flow of images and products, offers therapeutic religion, and mixes 'codes' from assorted elements of contemporary and secular culture. He obscures traditional lines of distinction between the secular and sacred, emphasizes personal experience over doctrinal constraints, and supports denominational independence over church hierarchy.[11]

The entrepreneurial, post-modernist, and therapeutic content are interwoven in Jakes' sermons.[12] Like many preachers in the "new black church," Jakes' ministry is multivalent and multimedia. In addition to serving as the pastor of a congregation of 30,000 members, Jakes also hosts conferences attended by hundreds of thousands each year, writes books, produces gospel records, writes and produces movies, and more. This plethora of entrepreneurial activity common to the postmodernist preacher, Lee alleges, fuels what some "fear that religion may be denigrating into just another business enterprise and [Jakes'] blend of religion and capitalism rouses many doubts about our nation's spiritual direction."[13]

Jakes' sermons illustrate a constant message about spiritual authority, especially his own authority to preach, as critical a resource for personal transformation. For example, Jakes begins his sermons with the words, "You may be seated in the presence of the Lord." On behalf of God, Jakes gives the congregation permission and instruction on proper reverence in God's presence a vital part of the formula needed to receive God's instruction and blessing for personal advancement. Jakes' spiritual authority is also reflected in his proclamation to be speaking as directed by God,

> I am sent to preach to somebody tonight . . . This is a word directly to your situation because the Lord wants to tell you of the things that will happen in the days to come.[14]

*T. D. Jakes*, 4.

Most of Jakes' sermons are presented in collections, based on sermon themes, and do not reflect the original date preached. Therefore, the sermons studied here are not necessarily presented in any chronological order.

*T. D. Jakes*, 7.

Jakes, "Get in the Birth Position."

> There is a shift that God has ordained for your life, [and] that if you can embrace the things that I am getting ready to share and bring your life into alignment with God's purpose and plan, there's going to be a shifting and repositioning in your life . . . God is go ing to do something awesome in your life.[15]

In the Economy of Power preaching paradigm, much of the ministe rial authority which engenders high degrees of trust is derived from claims of having been sent by God to deliver specific messages to the people. ditionally, the message urges black worshipers to adopt and adhere to all that the preacher outlines in order to access the healing, liberation, and abundance God has made possible for their lives.

> I want to define what God means when he says, "Leading lady" . . . You have the right to choose how you live the life that God has given you. It's an important choice, and you have to choose to live it God's way, or you'll get in the way of the destiny that God has for you. I have seven simple points that will make you a leading lady.

Despite his formulaic approach to personal transformation, Jakes' sermons in this preaching model reflects a dialectic tension which and Mamiya contend is common in the overall black preaching tradition— that is, on one hand, reliance upon God's justice and, on the other, an insis tence in individual personal responsibility. The message is: God will fight the battles and heal or correct what is wrong in worshipers' lives if they will align themselves in proper position to God.

> We are listening to Jesus in a discussion in the secret chambers of his presence with his disciples. And he's teaching them something I'm not sure the church has totally learned today. He's teaching them relationship . . . If you don't understand your place in the kingdom you might try to do something that only God can do . . . We are trying to heal ourselves, solve our own problems . . . We are standing in like a substitute teacher, trying to make God look good through our own human efforts, and it cannot be done . . . You don't have to move it, God will move it. You don't have to straighten it out, God will straighten it out. You don't have to fix it, God will fix it.
>
> God is there with you in the battle. You don't have to do it by your self . . . Being passive, saying 'the battle is not yours' it's the is a welcome mat to procrastinators . . . to relieve ourselves of the

15. Jakes, "Repositioning: The Message."

16. Jakes, "The Leading Lady," God's Leading Ladies Conference (2002).

17. Jakes, "Chosen," *Classics*, Vol. 1.

responsibility for engagement . . . I am not saying that you should do nothing but pray . . . You have to get engaged and you have to do something in order to win . . . The hardest thing in the world to do is to balance between what is my responsibility and what is God's responsibility . . . So the first thing I have to do is to recognize God . . . The second thing is to distribute responsibilities appropriately . . . But don't expect your old ideas about God to show up in your new situations . . . A narrow, myopic vision of God limits your understanding to thinking that God is a butler or maid that you can summons for your agenda . . . And the Lord says, 'I'm neither for you nor against you. It's about you being for me.[18]

lthough Jakes urges his audience to expand their thinking about how God will manifest in their lives, using his authority as spokesman for God, he establishes the parameters for how God manifests and operates in people's lives. He suggests that "your old ideas about God" are not sufficient to address the situations of people's lives, but that his ideas about God are. Jakes contends that what he expresses about how God moves and is ready to manifest are not merely his "ideas about God" but revelation about God that is from God. This kind of liturgical/rhetorical language may point to an argument made by both Marcia Riggs and James Harris that preachers often reinterpret scripture to align it with their own worldviews, and then present those as "the word of God."

In this preaching paradigm, there is no invitation to individuals to use their own spiritual authority to discern what God may be speaking. Borrowing from Iris Marion Young's argument that "cultural imperialism" is present when one individual or group "defines" a task that others are expected to "execute," Jakes reflects a ministerial imperialism that sets a stage for the preacher to define the parameters of spiritual life and for the churchgoers to live within those parameters as defined for them.

nother dialectic tension indicated in sermons of the Economy of Power paradigm emerges from one teaching that followers need to be chastised and rebuked in order to be able to hear God speak in their lives and another indicates that they would not have the desire to follow God if they had not heard and responded to God's call. This dialectic tension not only heightens worshipers' receptivity to what Brock refers to as "symbolic inducements," such as anointing and blessing from God, but is also a precursor to spiritual ambiguity and psychological anxiety within worshipers,

Jakes, "The Battle."

by fostering an anxiety about how much chastisement is sufficient in order to hear God speak and to received God's anointing.

> Father, we want your anointing to permeate this room, to saturate us, to impart life to us, to change us, to inspire us, to motivate us, to correct us, chastise us, to minister to us. We are available to your word for reproof, rebuke with all long suffering . . . Our only fear is that we won't hear from you. For if we don't hear from you, we won't know what to do to . . . Amen.[19]

Noting the dualisms and dichotomies in Jakes, Lee alleges, "Not unlike most powerful men and women, Jakes is a complicated individual brim ming with paradoxes and contradictions. There is Jakes the feminist juxta posed to Jakes the sexist. There is Jakes the liberationist alongside Jakes the conservative capitalist."[20]

While much of his ministry focuses on spiritual, emotional, and eco nomic empowerment, Jake sermons also reflect a strong political and social conservatism. This social conservatism and constrictivism are reflected in the following sermon about how to prepare for the realization of a life's dream or calling into which he weaves a strong invective against abortion. The two are interwoven in a way that suggests that not to allow any "seed" within to be realized is a violation against God.

> God is a God of seed. . . Words are powerful. . .if a word goes out it will produce something. . . We are dealing with the embryos that have been planted with words. . . When nothing else works, God uses some man or woman. . .[through] the foolishness of preach ing. . .without any other therapy, just a word from God. . . Just his word. . .and you can't get drunk enough to abort his word. . . This text is written to Israelite women who wanted to be pregnant, and we live in a culture of women who don't. . . Every time a woman had a baby, she felt like 'I am helping the miracle come to pass. . . They were not trying to pass legislation so they could kill their ba bies. . . We need in the church today of people are so eager to pro duce the promise of God that they say, 'Lord, give me the promise lest I die. . . I want something to pass through me that's greater than me, that's lasting and eternal. . . Give me a child. . .There's a calling, there's a gift, there's a ministry. . . And whatever I got to go through, I've got to produce life.[21]

19. Jakes, "Chosen" *Classics*, Vol. 1.

20. Lee, *T. D. Jakes*, 4. For example, Jakes' economic progressivism and political con servatism has fostered his close association with the Bush White House.

21. Jakes, "Get in the Birth Position." Scriptural text: Isaiah 54:1–6.

conomy of Power emphasizes financial prosperity and large-scale ministry activities, yet there is virtually no commentary given to social ills or to individual or aggregate Christian responsibility to help address those societal problems. The focus is almost exclusively on individual challenges and the application of spiritually-based strategies to address them. This preaching model also suggests that some challenges in life are ordained by God, and therefore, the goal is not to resolve the challenge or adversity, but to determine how to align with God in such a way that the lessons and strengthening intended from the adversity are accomplished. Once this alignment is complete, Jakes contends, God will remove the adversity.

> It's interesting to note that when evil comes . . . God will use evil to convey good . . . God monitors how much evil comes into my day . . . Some of you who have been praying for conditions on your job to get better, you may be praying against the purpose that God has for your life. God may be using the adversity on your job to create an atmosphere for you to fulfill your destiny . . . Many times God will put you in a situation that is not comfortable so that He might fulfill His purpose . . . God used that hostile environment to create a blessing for one of his children . . . This is a message not just for churchgoers, but for. . .those anointed by Christ . . . You're asking the job to give you something that your job is not designed to do . . . the job can't anoint you . . . Understand that God anointed you in trouble, not from trouble . . . To be anointed literally means to be empowered . . . You are strongest when life is challenging.[22]

nlike Taylor's sermons which frame God as *using* life adversities to strengthen and empower individuals in their spiritual and moral authority, sermons within the Economy of Power model portray God as *sending* adversities. By focusing on individual life struggles, Jakes does not address the implications or reasons for adversities and injustices occurring in the lives of groups of individuals. With the focus on individuals, Jakes uses language commonly associated with social justice movements and applies it to individual situations. Jakes' sermons generally do not examine the intersections between personal experiences and social realities, nor address the causes or consequences of those intersections except in relation to personal economic situations.

> Many of us came to Christ not only were we wounded because we were sinners, but wounded because we had been sinned against. . . Your personal sins are remitted at the cross of Calvary, but the after

Jakes, "10 Commandments of Working in a Hostile Environment."

effects of the damage that has been done to you having been sinned against continues to linger in your life. . . God specifically allows you to go through certain things to purge you of the negative influ ences that have affected your life. . . What is this thing that makes it difficult for us to break our tie with identifying with our oppres sor?. . . The challenge is when you have defined yourself. . .through a codependent relationship or issues or area or bondage. . .or a simple thing like poverty. . . People will not give themselves permission to prosper because they are accustomed to seeing themselves as poor. . . You can be hooked on pain, hooked on poverty. . . Because you have come to define yourself by your past situation.[23]

In this sermon, Jakes addresses the issue of money in the black community,

There is $200 billion in the African American community alone. They're sitting up now trying to figure out, 'What kinds of prod ucts can we make to get that $200 billion?' You need to be strat egizing, 'What kinds of investments can I come up with to keep my money?'. . . Most people live apathetically, numb, victimized. Having lost power they live as if their circumstances are not alterable. But you have the power to reposition many areas of your life. You can't alter the divine purpose for your life and the destiny that God has over your life, but there are many variables between where you are and what God has called you to do that are incidentals, that are totally up to you. . . Part of being like God is being a strategist. . . God has short-range and long-range goals. . . I refuse to pastor a people who do not think. . . Success is intentional. Nobody succeeds by accident.[24]

Jakes conveys his beliefs, shaped by his own life experiences that: God has a destiny for your life, 2) destiny includes for you to be prosperous and successful, including financially, 3) the primary limitations on the suc cess and prosperity in your life stem from your own thoughts about what is possible for you and your failure to align with God's will for your life, if you change your thinking and become aligned with God's purpose and plan for your life, you will change your life, and 5) your spiritual maturity is manifest by the degree of success and prosperity in your life. Characteristic of this paradigm, Jakes presents his beliefs as if they are they are a definitive

23. Jakes, "Frustration of Liberation."

24. Jakes, "Position Yourself to Prosper," sermon excerpt used as a promotional com mercial in "Defeating the Giant of Debt."

word from God absent any direct acknowledgement of how those beliefs are also informed by the preacher's worldview.

Jakes uses his ministerial authority and "symbolic inducement", declaring that "I will not pastor" individuals "who do not think" strategically and intentionally in order to succeed. Because of the clergy-congregant bond, the suggestion "I refuse to pastor you unless you comply with certain conditions" serves to induce, and even manipulate, congregants to follow the instruction of their pastor.

In addition to his ecclesiastical authority as a pastor, Jakes' authority is also deeply rooted in his charisma as a powerful preacher and a successful entrepreneur. His charismatic authority is the major element directing the clergy-congregant relationship between Jakes and his congregation and broader audiences. An example of a strong congregational trust is the relocation of fifty families with Jakes from Charleston, West Virginia to Dallas, Texas to help Jakes expand his ministry. That these families chose to move their households and change their jobs and children's schools indicates the degree of these congregants' allegiance to their pastor and in his spiritual authority.

Jakes' overall message about authority, charisma, and trust is inextricably tied to a belief in individual divine destiny. That is, the particular authority and charismatic gifts that individuals have are reflections of the plan that God has for their individual lives. God's designed plan, according to Jakes, is only activated by faith and action on the part of each individual. Because of a divine destiny, his argument would suggest, God gives higher degrees of authority to some individuals who God uses as the models and teachers for others.

## Patriot and Prosperity Preaching

Because of its limited social focus, the Economy of Power preaching model does not nurture, but instead narrows the moral compasses of black Christians. Marvin McMickle posits that many black preachers are what he refers to as patriot and prosperity preachers, who focus their sermonic themes on limited issues. He argues, "*patriot preachers* limit their messages to the issues of sexuality and abortion, [and] *prosperity preachers* limit their agenda to the single focus on the personal gain of individual believers."[25] McMickle

McMickle, *Where Have All the Prophets Gone?* 118. Also see Mitchem, *Name It*, ix.

contends that patriot and prosperity preachers operate from a "royal con
sciousness," reflecting deeply ingrained political, economic, social and reli
gious constructs of the status quo.[26] Patriot and prosperity preaching gives
limited significance to mission and social justice. In place of mission to the
society and world, emphasis is given to "money and the formula through
which that money can come into a person's life."[27]

According to McMickle, the lifestyles of wealth and prosperity of pa
triot and prosperity preachers signal their authority given by God to teach
and lead the people. Their success and wealth serve as confirmations of
what they preach.[28] Thus, their success, and therefore, their authority are
understood as the correct application of their authority from God. Jakes re
flects both patriot and prosperity preaching as characterized by McMickle.

Because of his almost exclusive emphasis on *personal* emotional heal
ing, spiritual growth, and financial gain, this model of preaching does not
contribute to black Christians' recognition of linkages between the chal
lenges in individual lives and systemic social problems. Further, it does not
inspire black congregants to participate in efforts to transform unjust social
systems and structures. Although Economy of Power sermons, at times,
address the adverse impacts of racial and other forms of social oppression
upon success and prosperity, their thrust is on what is possible in the lives
of individuals who align themselves with God's plan, despite the social bar
riers. Advancement is framed solely as a personal responsibility.

With a focus on individual success and acquisition,
Power reinforces what Brock refers to as a "national rhetoric" which values
personal gain over community welfare. The sermon messages are largely
sent from an individual preacher to individual worshipers, and not to them
as a corporate body. The action that worshipers are inspired or induced
to engage in the world is not through collective action nor on behalf or in
support of others, but rather to claim and manifest God's blessings in their
individual lives. There is an implicit message that the overall society will be
enriched as individual black worshipers, who align themselves with God by
the prescribed strategies and formulas, achieve God's blessings. This tiered
approach for receiving God's blessings constitutes a spiritual "trickle down"
theory of grace, healing, and liberation.[29]

26. McMickle, *Where Have All the Prophets Gone?* 11.

27. Ibid., 105.

28. Ibid., 112–13.

29. Jakes' sermons hint at the efficacy of "trickle down" economic theory, political

# Community Empowerment

That the Negro Church antedates the Negro home, leads to an explanation of much that is paradoxical in this communistic institution and in the morals of its members. But especially it leads us to regard the institution as peculiarly the expression of the inner ethical life of a people in a sense seldom true elsewhere.[1]

THE COMMUNITY EMPOWERMENT MODEL of black preaching focuses on the empowerment of worshiping communities to use their individual and collective human agency to foster personal and social justice-oriented transformation. This approach seeks to accomplish this by: 1) proclaiming a divinely bestowed authority that is shared by the community, 2) using sermonic language that affirms the unique gifts within the community to meet global needs, and 3) critiquing social issues within the black church, black communities, as well as in the broader national and global contexts.

This approach emerges from an understanding of scripture that black Christians are called into mutual responsibility and accountability and to be co-laborers with God in revealing a vision of world in which God's children, all humanity, experience the love and justice of God.

---

rhetoric which espouses that if the wealthy do well, benefits will "trickle down" to the ne example of this theory is the policy position that lower taxes on high income or capital gains will ultimately benefit most of the population because the wealthy will then be able to purchase goods and services the provision of which creates jobs for middle and low-income workers. See Aghion and Bolton, "Theory of Trickle-Down Growth and Development," 151–72.

Du Bois, "Souls of Black Folk" in *Writings*, 499.

As a part of the community with a distinctive role within the com
munity, preachers do not speak to the community as those who are more
enlightened, closer to God, or elevated above the congregation.
preachers exercise their authority along *with* the people, not
inspire them to operate in their full authority as well. Although sermons in
the Community Empowerment model exercised authority and charisma,
the congregational trust that is garnered is not based primarily on either
of these elements of power. Rather, trust is greatly fostered by sermons that
inspire black churchgoers to envision and appropriate for themselves what
they accomplish together, using biblical examples of what individuals and
communities can accomplish by the power of God at work in their lives.

This approach is distinctively prophetic as it proclaims the will of God
for the community to engage in honest, soul-searching introspection about
their relationship with God and God's people, and then to share in a critical
moral response based on what their soul searching reveals. Prophetic call
is demonstrated as a central emphasis on critiquing and challenging the
black church as well as the overall society to participate in reforming and
transforming social systems and structures as needed to bring about God's
justice. The prophetic approach is rooted in a scriptural understanding that
the social and the political are spiritual, as framed in Jesus's word, "What
ever you do unto the least of these, you do unto me."[2]

## Vashti Murphy McKenzie

Illustrating this preaching paradigm is Bishop Vashti Murphy Mc
Bishop McKenzie is a risk-taker whose courage is rooted in her trust in
God and in her love and compassion for people. Her willingness to take
bold risks has not only been the hallmark of her ministry in that it has
placed her in one trailblazing position after another, but has also been a
resource enabling her to facilitate the spiritual growth and healing of many
individuals within her denomination and beyond.

McKenzie's sermons emphasize an invitation to black churchgoers to
recognize the power and authority of God that is available for their lives, and
a call to them to activate that power to help heal and transform the world.
McKenzie's overarching message reflects the purposes of black preaching
indicated by Forbes: 1) following the model of Jesus, to prophetically lift up
a vision of justice, hope, peace, and love for all people; 2) nurture spiritual

2. Matthew 25:25.

experiences that empower black Christians to work as co-laborers with God to transform the world; and 3) offer a serious critique of the culture to attend to the needs of the global community.[3]

enzie was born in Baltimore, Maryland in 1947 into a well-known, community-leading family. She is named after her maternal grandmother, Vashti Turley Murphy, who was one of the founders of Delta Sigma Theta Sorority, Inc. McKenzie is also the granddaughter of Carl Murphy, editor and publisher of the *Afro-American* newspapers. As an undergraduate stu-

enzie enrolled at Morgan State University, a historically black university in Baltimore, where she majored in history. Later, she transferred niversity of Maryland in College Park, Maryland where she graduated with her bachelor's degree in journalism.

fter graduation, she began working for her family newspaper and wrote her own column, "The McKenzie Report." McKenzie began her career in radio broadcasting at WYCB Radio, hosting an afternoon drive Gospel show, and later becoming program director. McKenzie also worked as an on-air personality, program director, general manager for WJZ-TV, EBB and WAYE. She became Corporate Vice President of Programming for Mortenson Broadcasting Company.

Much of McKenzie's life, even prior to entering ordained ministry, has shaped within her both a deep compassion for all people and strong sense of social responsibility that are integral to her understanding of what it means to be a Christian.

enzie was raised attending an Episcopal Church. As a young adult, she joined Bethel A.M.E. Church in Baltimore, returning home to the Murphy family's original church. It was there, that she began experiencing a spiritual awakening and then sensing a call to ordained ministry. Before answering this call, McKenzie used her professional ties in broadcasting to engage in community service work, driven by a deep compassion for people. For a time, she thought this would be enough.

The call to ministry continued to stir in her heart. In the 1970s, enzie responded to a call from God for her to enter ordained ministry. She was ordained an itinerant deacon in the African Methodist piscopal Church in 1981, and served as pastor of two churches in Maryland—Bethel A.M.E. in Cecil County and Ebenezer A.M.E. Ordained as a reverend by the A.M.E. Church in 1984, McKenzie was appointed pastor ak Street A.M.E. Church.

Forbes interview, January 22, 2002.

As part of her preparation for ministry, McKenzie earned her master of divinity degree from Howard University Divinity School in Washington D.C. and earned a doctor of ministry degree from United Theological Seminary in Dayton, Ohio.

In 1990, McKenzie was appointed pastor at Payne Memorial Baltimore. In 1997, a poll of national leaders selected McK magazine's "Honor Roll of Great African American Preachers." Mc serves as a member of President Barack Obama's Religious Council and the National Chaplain for Delta Sigma Theta Sorority, Inc. She is the author of four books: *Not Without a Struggle, Strength in the Struggle: Leadership Development for Women, A Journey to the Well*, and *Swapping Housewives: Rachel and Jacob and Leah.*

McKenzie serves as the 117th elected and consecrated bishop of the African Methodist Episcopal (A.M.E.) Church. Her historic election in the year 2000 represents the first time in the over 200-year history of the Church, in which a woman had obtained that level of Episcopal office. In 2011, she again made history becoming the first woman to become the Titular Head of the A.M.E. denomination, as the president of the Council of Bishops, making her the highest-ranking woman in the predominately Black Methodist denominations. McKenzie currently serves as the presiding prelate of the 13th Episcopal District which includes Tennessee and Kentucky. Previously, she served in 2000–2004 as the chief pastor of the 18th Episcopal District in Southeast Africa, which is comprised of Swaziland, Botswana and Mozambique.

McKenzie effectively integrates her media career with her ministry as she uses a poetic preaching style that speaks to the spiritual, social, and moral issues of the day. She also uses the cultural linguistic style common among black women as she, at times, addresses issues in a somewhat direct, yet coded way. Doing so enables McKenzie to take the risks of addressing issues that might be unpopular or out of the traditional boxes of the discourse within black churches. For example, immediately before preaching, McKenzie prayed:

> Oh Mother God . . . We are no longer, woman, no longer mother, but the embodiment of the power of God . . . Take us where we've never been, speak what we've never heard before, reveal what we have never seen before.[4]

4. McKenzie, "From Mess to Miracle: Hold on Hagar."

ddressing legislative actions under way in 2010–2012 by conserva-
epublican Party politicians constricting the rights of women's health
decisions, McKenzie urges,

> My sisters . . ., we's under attack in the most subtle and overt ways
> of control and manipulation . . . Don't sleep through this.[5]

While McKenzie is bold in using her spiritual authority to challenge
black worshipers, she does not use language that is often characteristic
of many black preachers, such as "God sent me by her to tell you." Even
without this overt proclamation of spiritual authority, McKenzie uses her
er charismatic presence and poetic communication along with
the trust that she inspires in her audiences are sufficient for her to use an
authority from God that she tells others that they too have. McKenzie challenges black churchgoers to acknowledge the ways in which the contemporary church has become like the religious hegemony of Jesus' time.

> Jesus confronted the status quo with his good news . . . Most of the
> time when we come to church, we are looking for confirmation, not
> confrontation . . . We're looking for something to affirm what we
> already believe. We are not looking for our belief systems to be as-
> saulted or confronted . . . But when Jesus speaks of the good news
> e is not proclaiming the status quo as sacred but is proclaiming
> a new message . . .
> When we come to church, we preach and teach, but not what
> he preached. If you preach what Jesus preached. . .what happened
> to Jesus will also happen to you. For the church folk . . . the leading
> religious authorities of the day did to him what we do to anybody
> who dares to tell us the truth. We get so mad, we want to kill them.[6]

She urges black churchgoers to open their hearts and minds to participate in changes within the church and society to meet needs today.
This urging expresses McKenzie's hermeneutic that the people of God
need not be victims of change or resisters of it but are called to be change
agents, like Jesus.

> Change happens . . . as new realities emerge . . . Change doesn't
> seek our cooperation. Formidable moments can happen to indi-
> viduals or nations . . . How we perceive the change dictates how we
> respond to it . . . Many of us view change as a threat . . . Jesus was

enzie, "Let's Build Bridges Together."

criticized because he was about change . . . Jesus is a change agent
. . . When you give your life, old things pass away and all things
become new . . . He changed the wages of sin with the gift of life . . .
If Jesus is a change agent . . . then how come we have such a hard
time with change?[7]

The Community Empowerment model urges black churchgoers to
reflect on the self-interests of comfort and community for which Chris
tians often come to church, and challenges them to open themselves to be
confronted and transformed by the experience of worship.

Why do you come to church? And what do you expect to get out of
it? Do you come to be comforted, or do you come to be confronted?

In telling the story of the Mt. Everest climbers who stopped to save
the life of climber Lincoln Hall, who had been stranded and left for dead,
McKenzie pushes the congregation to reflect on the God who calls us to
think beyond our own personal interests to help others, even those we do
not know and with whom we have no direct relationship.

Which one of us would turn our back on a dream and sacrifice
something so important that you set aside money and time and
took years to prepare for? Which one of us would set aside your
dream so that somebody else could live?
Standing at the "fork in the road" decision. It's either them or
me. Us or them. And how would you make the decision?
century culture does not support that kind of thing. We live in the
days of great indulgence and self-indulgence. Our world is a world
of "take care of me." "I got mine, you got to get yours.[9]

Community Empowerment sermons seek not only to move black
churchgoers beyond a focus on individual self-interest but also beyond
an emphasis on the black community alone. Her preaching is consistent
with the traditional focus of black preaching as what Henry Mitchell re
fers to as a "unique response" to the historic racism that shapes much of
black experience, yet is not her singular focus. With this expanded focus,
McKenzie moves from traditional preaching that fosters a sense of victim
hood and marginalization to more empowerment and authority. She calls
black Christians to be agents for global changes that are needed to heal and

7. McKenzie, "Favor Makes a Difference," 2009.
8. McKenzie, "Fork in the Road Decisions," 2009.
9. Ibid.

transform the world, rooted in the scriptural the paradox that as we help heal the world, we are healed. This emphasis signals that black Christians have the individual and collective power to make changes.

> If your first concern is to look after yourself, you're going to lose yourself and you'll never find yourself. But if you lose yourself, you'll find yourself. And if you want to lead somebody, then you have to serve . . .
>
> There will always be fork-in-the-road decisions between what you want and what needs to be done. Between what needs to be done and what is best to be done. Between what you can afford to do and what you cannot afford to let go. Between a common agenda and political agenda. Between what you want to include and whom you must include. Between blaming a victim and blaming a pattern of structural violence . . . Fork in the road decisions between those who have resources and those who have [only] some or none.[10]

In challenging the "normative ideals" present in black church culture, Community Empowerment sermons lay the groundwork for what Iris Marion Young refers to as developing an "alternative vision of social relations" needed for justice. Unlike many sermons in this contemporary era that focus almost exclusively on how to appropriate the power of God primarily for individual interests, McKenzie urges,

> We can no longer sit passively under our respective. . .pomegranate trees. We must become proactive in our communities to be sure that . . . every child has enough to eat, old folks can live their last days with security . . . Saul contented himself under his mega-pomegranate tree. He was afraid of losing what he had gained and so he sat contented. How many of us today...are willing to fold our arms and sit contentedly under our pomegranate trees while the world goes to hell in a hand basket?[11]

There is tremendous power available as we walk with God. But that power, according to McKenzie is not only for the individual Christian alone, but to be garnered also to help others. Power and authority are available from God not only in a pyramidal system beginning with pastors with a trickle down to the rank and file congregants. But power and authority is conferred to all who take the risk of trusting God.

> The equation of power and authority is reconfigured because of
> the favor of God. Power and authority are transferred to those who
> are favored by God right under the noses of those who think they
> have power and authority . . . The captive (Joseph) became the
> captain . . . The one who was in prison became in charge of the
> prisoners . . . transferring power and authority. . . He would make
> decisions rather than having decisions made for him . . .
>
> Favor will put you in a place where you can't put yourself
> . . . The favor of God is not diminished or weakened by the nega
> tive actions of others . . . We live in an uncertain world, uncertain
> times. . . .but the favor of God has the power to prosper you even in
> a recession . . . [It was] the favor of the Lord that caused [Joseph]
> to prosper in the pit, the prison and palace.[12]

For Community Empowerment, to operate in the full power of God
requires courage, patience and trusting in God. It is through this kind rela
tionship of with God that Christians are empowered.

> We pray "God grant us peace," only to learn that peace is best taught
> in turmoil. . . We pray for courage, and we find that courage is de
> veloped on the battlefield. . . We pray for patience only to learn that
> patience is learned in waiting and waiting some more. . .We expect
> a return on our belief only to find out that it's only when our beliefs
> are tested and tried that we find out what we really believe...

McKenzie takes risks to send challenges to the status quo church lead
ers again and again. Such challenges reflect the prophetic call of the Com
munity Empowerment model.

> When we build barriers "Whosoever will" becomes "whosoever I
> like. . . [or] whosoever agrees with me". . . We [must] go beyond the
> comfort zones of our sanctuaries, our homes and our neighbor
> hoods to take the power of God. . .and to those who are outside of
> the household of faith. . . How can we build a bridge over troubled
> water, when we haven't built a bridge to each other in here? You
> gotta build a bridge to each other in here, so that when those out
> there come in they won't fall between the cracks. . .in here.

In her sermons, books, and blogs, McKenzie seeks to equip black
Christians and others to be effective leaders in helping to heal and transform

12. McKenzie, "Favor Makes a Difference."
13. McKenzie, "From Mess to Miracle: Hold on Hagar."
14. McKenzie, "Let's Build Bridges Together."

the world. For McKenzie, the purpose of leadership is to help others live with more dignity, authenticity, and wholeness.

> egacies require moving beyond short-term definitions of leadership success. To leave a lasting legacy, one must move success to significance. To be a leader. . .brings with it the responsibility to do something of significance that makes our families, our communities, our work organizations, our country, the environment, and the world a better place than they are today.[15]
>
> In facing an uncertain future, Jonathan moved with confidence. . .because he was dependent on God and not himself. . . He risked exposure in a place where he was most vulnerable, and God granted him the victory. But he still had to fight the battle, and so must we. . .. [Jonathan's] leadership and motion encouraged other people to act. . . They found their courage because they saw one. . . h, the power of one. . .[16]

ecognizing that it takes a strong sense of self to be an effective leader who participates in transforming the world, Community Empowerment sermons encourage black churchgoers to claim their spiritual power and authority. McKenzie urges that to do so, Christians must go beyond two tendencies common in black church communities—one, a need for affirmation and accolades and two, a focus on trying "to fit in" by being like someone else.

> Jesus didn't come to just make a name for himself. . . He was indifferent to the appearance and accolades of humankind. . .
>
> Listen, listen, listen, [they] chose personal integrity over public popularity. . . John [the Baptizer] was serious about his role. . .Jesus was serious about saving his people. . . God used different means and methods and persons to free humanity from sin, death, and hell. Each [Jesus and John] was not a carbon copy of the other. Each used different methodologies and strategies to fulfill the ministry that God had called them to. If we understand this, then we won't try to preach like somebody else preaches. . .or teach like somebody else teaches.
>
> God created us unique, not to be a carbon copy of somebody else. . . God has given you unique gifts and skills and talents. . .so that you would shine in the places where God has put you.[17]

> enzie, "Seven Steps: One Step at a Time."
> enzie, "Fork in the Road Decisions."
> enzie, "People Pleasers."

The Community Empowerment paradigm emphasizes that every hu man being, as directed by the power of God, has the responsibility and the ability to participate in the healing and transforming the church, their neighborhoods, workplaces, and the world.

> Who will dare to climb the cliffs of public policy and inspire a nation to rise out of the dust of dwindling civil liberties and fear to confront the tough issues of our country?[18]

To engage in the work of transformation, McKenzie suggests, requires Christians who are bold enough to be guided by God and not by positions or titles conferred by the church leaders or others. Directly addressing the issues of "cultural imperialism," McKenzie reminds black Christians that Jesus did not model supporting systems of oppression in the religious com munity, but illustrated a life of interrupting those systems so that the work of God could be realized more fully.

> [Jesus] didn't spend time "kissing up" to the Pharisees or "brown-nosing" to the Sadducees . . . There's nothing in the scripture that he was sucking up to Pilate, or Herod, or the pastor. Excuse me, I'm sorry.[19]
>
> Sometimes it's hard to decide which way to go . . . Now give us the strength, the courage, and the faith to seek the way you would have us go . . . Help us to go the right way even if it costs us our reputations, our names, our titles, and our resources. help us when we have to make such a decision.[20]

A central activity within the Community Empowerment model is interrupting oppressive socioethical values and practices while simultane ously promoting a new vision of both black church and the global com munities. Community Empowerment directly confronts the realities of exclusionism based on race, gender and other factors. H spiritual strategies used by Joshua and the people of Israel to break through the walls of Jericho, McKenzie urges black Christians to develop spiritual strategies to breakthrough all forms of social oppression and impenetrable situations.

> How do we get in when no one wants us in? ... How do we get in behind closed doors? . . . How do we get in. . ., especially when

18. McKenzie, "Fork in the Road Decisions."

19. McKenzie, "People Pleasers."

20. McKenzie, Closing prayer, "The Way In."

everyone wants us to stay out? . . . [You] have to have a methodol-

Assemble the resources . . . [It] requires a risk-taking faith . . .
We often lead with secular [strategies] trying to heal the spiritual,
and wonder why it doesn't work . . .

The strategy. Lead with your spiritual discipline. God up front
. . . [For Joshua and Israel] it required a discipline. The people who
had been silent for six days, then now they were to shout. Praising
God was the solidifier. [The] secret weapon was faith . . . Faith to
believe otherwise.

[People ask:] How did you get elected to the Council of Bishops of the African Methodist Episcopal Church after 200 years? . . .

ll I did was take a risk to stand in the place of opportunity and
God got me in.[21]

Sermons within the Community Empowerment paradigm seek to expand the thinking of black churchgoers beyond defining themselves based
on their life circumstances and personal wounding to identifying with Jesus
who reappropriates and redefines his wounds as signs of life and victory.

Jesus shows us a different way to think about the wounds we encounter in life . . . All of God's children have wounds. Some of us
suffer in silence. We camouflage our wounds . . . Some of us bleed
all over the place . . . to gain sympathy. . .

The weary and wounded, injured, tired . . . Wounded who
have resigned themselves to the wounding, thinking that they
have deserved it . . . Wounds getting in the way of our living everyday . . . Unlike most of us who are willing to hide our wounds,
Jesus shows his wounds . . .

His wounds were fulfillment of the Old Testament, "he was
wounded for our transgressions and bruised for our iniquity" . . .
The wounds themselves were a sign of healing . . . They identify
him with the human condition . . .

[The wounds] demonstrate that in spite of what happened
to him on Calvary it did not get in the way. The wounds of his de-
scent did not prevent his ascent . . . The wounds of his humiliation
did not prevent his elevation . . . The wounds of his crucifixion did
not get in the way of his glorification . . . If Jesus got up from his
wounds so shall we.[22]

In the Community Empowerment preaching model, preachers locate
themselves in the scriptural texts in ways that disclose their own human

enzie, "Don't Let Your Wounds Get in the Way."

struggles without attaching guilt and shame, thus, modeling and facilitat
ing for black churchgoers to do the same.

> In the midst of her hurt, in the midst of her hate . . . there is hope.
> Just to be able to see God in the midst of your problems . . .
> reminds you that God will act. All she had was a promise. She was
> sent back . . . There's a difference between being "sent back" and
> "went back" . . . To be sent back by God . . . that means God has
> an investment in the send. God is not going to send you without
> you being protected . . . There's a Hagar is in here. The situation
> hasn't changed . . . and God is sending you back . . . You have
> changed while you are here . . . Because you're going back with a
> different mind, different perspective. Not to respond like you used
> to . . . Rather than put your hands on your hip . . . you'll let Sarai's
> mess roll off you . . . Nothing Sarai could do to you . . .
> took the hate, the hurt . . . You've been shot, mistreated . . . You're
> still standing . . . You are still in the game, ain't nothing they can
> do. . . Ain't falling out, depressed, not going to run myself ragged
> . . . Not going to worry myself into early retirement. No, no, no.
> Why? Because you went out there and got some help. You heard
> God, you've seen God, and were sent back . . . God goes with you
> . . . In God's own time . . . a change is going to come.[23]

The story begins with Hagar, moves to the Hagars in the room, and
then includes McKenzie relating herself to those who want to leave harsh
situations, who see and talk with God, who are "sent back" by God, and who
go back changed and empowered. The way the story is told subtly conveys
the message that all people, even preachers, experience situations so hurtful
that they can produce hate. The story also conveys that all the
room can be sustained by hope to know that God has an investment in their
lives and will sustain them.

McKenzie reflects what James Harris refers to as "the being of the
preacher." In her sermon about the importance of trusting God to take
risks to "uncover new realities," she has tremendous credibility in this
invitation to take risks because her life, "the being of the preacher," dem
onstrate what new realities can be discovered and what new freedoms can
be experienced in God.

> Risk-takers may be valued but often not understood . . . We have a
> love-hate relationship with risk-takers . . . They take the risk for us
> . . . they show us that our cultural [realities] . . . can be otherwise . . .

23. McKenzie, "From Mess to Miracle."

They think otherwise . . . considered foolish and impractical . . . As soon as we have learned to master one thing, they come and bring something else . . . They make our standard bar. They raise the bar. They uncover new realities . . .

God created us to grow mentally, and emotionally, and physically through a life that takes us to the edge . . . Faith as risk-taking involves seeing what needs to be done, and then getting involved in it . . . We are God's people . . . Then we must be faith risk-takers as well. For God took a risk in creating human beings as free moral creatures . . .[24]

## Facilitative Preaching

ather than make herself the central actor who is sharing her wisdom, enzie presents herself as a facilitator who is helping the community see something more clearly that is already in the text. This facilitator role is a critical element of Community Empowerment that transforms not only the preaching experience but how sermons impact the lives of the hearers. Joshua in the scripture text is the principal actor, not the preacher. This act of de-centering accomplishes two important things: one, McKenzie models for back churchgoers how to read scripture to look for clues about how to live with victory in their daily lives, and two, she positions herself as a member of the community, not someone who is more spiritually enlightened and elevated. In the excerpt that follows, McKenzie's use of the *Joshua* shows *us* how to get in" is a critical example of how she de-centers herself even as she uses her spiritual authority.

The nature of the times we're living in with such fluidity of change. When the boundaries of understanding have been moved and limitations upon gender roles have been eliminated. And culture and society like to assign us roles and positions for us to fit into whether they have asked out permission or not . . . say, "here is where you'll stay." When you move from your assigned place, it causes such great tension in the atmosphere. So even though, you have gifts . . . skills and talents, experiences and wisdom . . . knowledge and prepared, there is a world that says you cannot be in. The walls have been fortified just like Jericho. Joshua shows us how to get in.[25]

enzie, "The Way In."

Community Empowerment sermons do not reflect the dialectic ten
sion that Lincoln and Mamiya observed in most black preaching. These
sermons are not focused merely on helping black churchgoers to engage
in survival activities, but also in pronouncing the liberative and trans
formative. These sermons are geared to helping people live rooted in the
power and freedom of God in the realm of this world. While the majority
of the sermons are preached in predominately black contexts and address
uniqueness of black culture and experiences, the sermons are intended
to bring universal messages of Christianity extended to all people.
center of the sermons is the message that the spiritual is woven through
every aspect of individual and collective lives.

# Under Submission

The theology of the average colored church is basing itself far too much upon 'Hell and Damnation'—upon an attempt to scare people into being decent and threatening them with the terrors of death and punishments. We are still trained to believe a good deal that is simply childish in theology. The outward and visible punishment of every wrong deed . . . the repeated declaration that anything can be gotten by anyone at any time by prayer."[1]

NDER SUBMISSION MODEL of black preaching proclaims that the power and authority of Jesus Christ are available to individuals who operate under the authority of their preachers. This model of preaching is based in a cultural imperialism that is marked by several key characteristics—a constant focus on issues of power and authority, emphasis on the preacher as the definitive priestly voice of God, disparagement of the congregation as spiritually immature, an almost exclusive favor and focus on one sub-group within the community (most often men), marginalization of other sub-groups within the community (generally women), and only nominal attention to broader social concerns.

Deeply rooted in the theology of apostolic succession, the overarching claim of Under Submission is that in order to live victoriously, black Christians must submit themselves under the authority of those whom God has appointed as their spiritual leaders. Within this approach, rituals and symbolic expressions serve to position preachers in the role of priests

Du Bois, "The New Negro Church" in *Against Racism*, 85.

with authority *over* the community.[2] Claiming divine authority, preachers operating within this approach not only instruct black churchgoers how to claim their own spiritual authority but also direct them regarding how to live all aspects of their lives.

This model reflects a dualistic tension regarding how individual spiritual authority is to be accessed and used. On one hand, it makes an insistent call to individuals to take authority over their life destinies; on the other hand, conversely, it also brings an insistent message that preachers are the definitive voice from God with the right to determine the acceptable ways for individuals to use their spiritual authority. Chastisement of congregants is frequently used as a tool to undergird the belief that the priest-preachers are the definitive reference point for how God is leading the community. Congregants are taught that some aspects of sermons are too spiritually profound for most worshipers to comprehend, and therefore, they need the preachers in order for them to grasp the full meanings of the messages from God.

This preaching model is also characterized by its thematic focus on a single life challenge, largely to the exclusion of other issues that may impact people's lives. While there is a very narrow thematic focus in most sermons, it is often presented in ways that uncritically link a host of other themes that are likely to evoke high emotional responses from black churchgoers. The sermons in the Under Submission preaching model offer a finite set of solutions to the narrow range of life challenges that they present.

## Eddie L. Long

This model for how authority, charisma, and trust are reflected in the black preaching tradition is illustrated in the preaching ministry of Bishop Eddie L. Long.

There is very little known about the personal life of Eddie to his years in the ministry. Long was born in North Carolina in Long received a Bachelor's degree in Business Administration from North

---

2. In their typology of dialectic pairs reflected in black preaching, Mamiya posit that all black churches engage in both priestly and prophetic functions. The priestly role emphasizes the worship activity and spiritual life of the community, and whereas the prophetic focuses more on God's judgment and liberation. See Mamiya, *Black Church in the African American Experience*, 12.

3. Long allows little information to be released regarding his upbringing or his life prior to entering the ministry. Therefore, the biographical information on Bishop is considerably less than on Taylor or Jakes.

Carolina Central University. After several years in the ministry, he completed a Master of Divinity degree from Interdenominational Theological

lthough a few years older than Jakes, Long considers Jakes his father and mentor in the ministry.[4]

1987, Long has served as the senior pastor of one of the nation's largest megachurches, New Birth Missionary Baptist Church in Lithonia, Georgia a suburb of Atlanta. Under Long's leadership, the church grew members to more than 30,000. Representative of post-modernist black preachers, Long is active in the "Baptecostal" movement, a subset of neo-Pentecostalism, that blends Baptist ecclesiastical polity and Pentecostal charismatic spirituality.[5] Long's television ministry is broadcast to more 170 countries around the world.

While little is known about Long's family background during his developmental years that helps understand what has shaped his theology of preaching, much of Bishop Long's life has become very public in recent ong made unfavorable headlines and controversy in 2010 when four young men in New Birth Missionary Baptist filed lawsuits against ong for sexual misconduct, alleging that he used his influence, trips, gifts, and jobs to coerce them into sexual relations with him.[6] Like Henry Lyons, ong adamantly denied any wrongdoing and he even likened his plight to that of David in a battle with Goliath.[7] But in May 2011, he reached an out-of-court settlement with these young men following months of mediation.[8] Shortly after this case was settled, Long settled another lawsuit filed by ten members of New Birth against him for his role in what turned out to be a real estate investment scam in which they collectively lost $1 million.[9]

ong, "Taking Authority of God's Word."

ong's church is affiliated with the Full Gospel Baptist Church Fellowship comprised of clergy and congregations from diverse historically black denominations including Baptist, Pentecostal, and Methodist. Long is one of the founding bishops, along with Bishop Paul Morton.

Eddie Long Case Officially Dismissed."

Untitled" sermon in response to allegations of (2010), "I am not the man who is being portrayed on television, that's not me. I've been accused, I'm under attacked.. But this thing, I'm gonna fight."

While many members left New Birth following the out-of-court settlement, there were many others who did not regard the settlement as an admission of guilt. One member ong is 'like a lot of movie-star preachers, arrogant and a bit puffed up,' butnot guilty of the accusations." Poole, "Eddie Long Case Officially Dismissed."

ong encouraged members of the church to invest in the venture, he stated, "I am responsible for everyone I bring before you and what they say." Long made this

Following these scandals, Long took a one-month leave of absence. Prior to taking his leave, Long stated, "I'm still your pastor. You'll still re ceive my direction." Upon his return to the pulpit at the New Year's Watchnight service, Long urged the congregation, "Shake off the remorse, shake off the depression, shake off the financial burden, start using your hands again and reconstructing! God is more about your future than he was about your past."[10]

Long made headlines news again in 2012 when he was declared "king" in a ceremony led by Messianic Jew and self-proclaimed rabbi er.[11] Messer proclaimed over Long, "He's a king. God's blessed him. a humble man. But in him is kingship. In him is royalty." During the cer emony, Messer directed men to lift Long up as he sat in a chair and to wrap a Torah scroll around him. This ceremony was received with applause from New Life congregants and posted on the official church website. The cer emony was later removed from the website once considerable outrage was made by Jewish groups, citing that there is no such ceremony in Judaism and that Messer had no right to make the claim that he had any religious authority to make this declaration.

Long's sermons used in this analysis span over one decade, and thus, do not allow for the observation of any shifts within the focus of his preach ing.[12] These sermons are among those identified by Long as some of his premiere sermons, thus, suggesting the kinds of messages he regards as important for his audience.

Long typifies a movement of black preachers, who in the focusing their ministries on empowering black men to be the "heads of their homes."[13] Long and others have used the power of the pulpit to ad

---

statement at the seminar, according to the lawsuit. "The gentleman that I am going to bring before you is an ordained minister. That gives me great pride to bring him for you." Steven, "Bishop Eddie Long Accused in Investment Scam."

10. Mohammed, "Bishop Eddie Long Back at New Birth Pulpit?"

11. Hunter, "Bishop Eddie Long Returns to the Pulpit."

12. Although Long's career in ministry spans over twenty-five years.

13. This movement, I believe, is in direct response to a several realities that have con tributed to a shift in the landscape of the black families and communities across the na tion: increasing numbers of two-income earning households, professional advancement of black women, growing number of women in ordained ministry, increasing numbers of black men going to prison, a shrinking population of black men due to drug violence and AIDS-related deaths, and increasing numbers of black men acknowledging their homosexuality and opting not to get married. Collectively, these changes in the black cultural landscape have been perceived as threats to what many black men regard as vital

dress what they perceive to be a critical issue impacting the black community—the role and welfare of black men.[14] Long has written several books
with titles such as *The Gladiator: Strength of a Man and Called to Conquer.*
While women have not been completely overlooked by Long, his focus remains on empowering men.[15] For example, he proclaims,

> ll creation is waiting for the sons and daughters to be a perfect
> man . . . God is raising up a corporate man . . . a corporate repre-
> sentation of God . . . the true body of Christ. . .the revealing of the
> true uncompromised body of Christ . . . the sons and daughters
> that stand up against the flood of the enemy . . . God has been
> calling for the corporate man since the original Garden.[16]

ong visually represents this emphasis on the power and authority
of men by preaching in sleeveless preaching robes that reveal his short-
sleeved muscle shirts and his well-developed arm muscles. Often when
about to make a critical point in his sermons to which he wants his audience to pay close attention, in a way that is unique to him, Long says, "Look
ook at me."

The focus of spiritual power as explained in the Under Submission
preaching model is largely on personal transformation, especially economic advancement. For example,

> 'Then you will be a special treasure to me above all people' . . .
> Those who used to rule us will now serve us. I'm not talking

---

conditions for the overall well-being and quality of life for black men, and therefore, the
black community.

During his tenure as senior pastor (1974–2009) of Saint Paul Community Baptist
Church in Brooklyn, New York, Rev. Johnny Ray Youngblood (now pastor emeritus),
referred to men as "seed-bearers." With the emphasis on the empowerment of men during that time, the church's ministerial staff was comprised entirely of men, and no women
ministers were invited as guest preachers. Now under the leadership of the current lead
ev. David K. Brawley, the focus of the men's ministry has expanded to: "The
ldad Medad Men's Ministry, an intentional ministry to Black men, which challenges
and empowers them to be strong leaders of our communities, Bible based vanguards who
are politically aware, involved in social action and are the cord that bonds family." Additionally, there is now a woman minster on the church staff, suggesting that perhaps the
church leadership is exploring ways to empower men without disempowering women.
ldad Medad Men's Ministry."

Such an emphasis on men in a system where men are already privileged in the
congregational hierarchy, sustains oppressive socioethical values and sociopolitical practices in black churches.

ong, "2006, the Year of the Man."

about people, but about systems . . . When you were born you accepted the mark of the beast which is the dollar . . . If we do it the way the system is set it up we'll give them more . . . But God says, 'your money is not supposed to work for the system, your money is supposed to work for you' . . . Say I'm chosen (I'm chosen), royal priesthood, a holy nation.[17]

The Under Submission paradigm is explicit in maintaining that authority is granted only through apostolic succession, or perhaps more accurately, through a type of spiritual pyramid system similar to the wealth-building systems used for generating passive income. In order for black Christians to have authority in their lives, as Long proclaims, they must submit to the authority of their pastors. This submission to him is viewed as a submission to God, who is the ultimate giver of authority. For example,

My father is Bishop T. D. Jakes, and it would be easy for me to rebel . . . I need to submit to him to have the authority . . . God will continue to bless you when you honor and submit to authority . . . I am a man under authority . . . When you're under authority, you have authority . . . When you rebel against delegated author ity, you're not rebelling against that man, but against God . . . The authority of God is the root struggle of all authority. . .in marriage, in government . . . We've . . . run from God's authority through psychology, science, and education with a false sense of belief that if we exalt our minds high enough we can be in charge . . . The highest price we pay in life for the rejection of God's authority is the chaos and confusion we're encountering today in our streets . . . We can operate in disobedience . . . and God says to you, 'My eyes are closed to you and I don't hear your prayers.'[18]

Under Submission employs the "call-and-response" preaching tech nique widely used in the black preaching tradition. While this practice is applauded both for facilitating therapeutic free expression and keeping alive a legacy of African culture, this practice also can be used as a technique for control. Although it can be argued that simply having the opportunity for expression can be therapeutic, it is questionable whether there is any inher ent therapeutic or empowering value in the specific words selected or in the frequency with which Long directs his congregation to repeat him, as illustrated in this sermon,

17. Long, "Conquer and Subdue."
18. Long, "Taking Authority of God's Word."

et them have dominion . . . Say 'Let them have' (Let them have) . . .
Say 'our dominion' (our dominion) . . . God never changed his mind.
Say 'never changed his mind' (never changed his mind). What God
is expecting of us, his sons and daughters . . . is that we grow up . . .
We are finding our place in the body. Say, 'finding our place' (finding
our place) . . . The greatest peace you can ever experience is to be
able to say, 'For this reason I was born' . . . No matter how deep you
were in depression, or deep you were in debts, or deep in a disgust-
ing lifestyle, God has given you dominion over it.[19]

In addition to proclaiming God as the source and giver of all authority, this preaching model emphasizes that it is only through the shed blood
of Jesus and the power of his resurrection that God's power and authority
become available to the people of God, not through ecclesiastical systems.

There's no power in this walk without the blood of Jesus . . . [Je-
sus says,] 'I have come that you might have this kind of life' . . . a
vitality and a spirit and a walk that is so powerful that it is conta-
gious. . . You cannot take my power . . . I woke up for a fight . . . to
declare the name of the Lord . . . I am empowered by God . . . 'I am
come that you might have life'. . .to possess vitality and the absolute
fullness of life both essential and ethical . . . I want you to grab your
portion in life, and cling to it, and let nobody take it from you.[20]

While it is difficult to assess what Long means here by "fullness of life
both essential and ethical," his sermon suggests that spiritual power and
moral authority come only from God, through the resurrection power of
Jesus Christ, and that this power is available to all who claim it in God. Long
declares that anyone who accesses the power of God in Jesus Christ will have
all that is needed for their lives. Power and authority come from God, but
are accessible only through submitting to "those who have charge over you."

With limited exception, Under Submission generally excludes direct
discussion of social ills and social justice activism to address those ills. As
ong notes in one sermon, part of his rationale for his support of a pro-
.S. Constitutional amendment[21] that would define marriage as only

ong, "Our Dominion."

ong, "Blood of Jesus and Its Power."

2004, as President George Bush and other politicians across the U.S. were
working toward a Marriage Amendment to the U.S. Constitution that would define marriage as only between a man and a woman and thus ban marriage equality, the Bush
ouse reached out to leading black preachers to enlist their support. Long responded to this appeal from Bush.

between a man and a woman, was that megachurches are criticized for not addressing substantive social issues. Long organized his congregation and other black ministers and churches from across the U.S. to participate in a protest march through the streets of Atlanta to declare their remonstration against marriage equality, as a moral issue. Long links this protest with a larger call to address major social needs, alleging that homosexuality, poverty, and inadequate health care, and education are all the result of spiritual attack. For example, the advertised purpose of the march was,

> to take a stand and make a statement of our belief that marriage is between one man and one woman. Other goals include programs that create wealth for the lesser privileged, the promotion of educational reform, and affordable health care . . . as God's children, we need to stand united in taking back what the enemy has stolen from us.[22]

On the night before the march, Long gives his rallying call to his congregation, suggesting that the march is a statement against systems that rob black Christians of the blessings God has available for them.

> We are coming out of silence, coming out of complacency, coming out of being ignored. Please understand, silence means agreement. Up until now, we have agreed with the stuff that's going on . . . One of the criticisms of megachurches is that we are not involved in civic matters . . . God has called us as strength in numbers . . . to call new birth, new revelation, new insight . . . We are concerned about what is going on in the wilderness . . . [God says:] 'Obey my voice.' Say 'my voice' (my voice) . . . This is a royal processional of God . . . We proclaim the praises of him who has called us out of darkness into the marvelous light . . . 'We once were scattered, but are now the people of God.'[23]

Long begins the sermon with one topic—the purpose of their gathering to prepare spiritually for the march proclaiming marriage as acceptable only between one man and one woman—then shifts to taking authority over finances, then back again to issues of sexuality, and then to being a people chosen by God. The sermon continues,

> What does God require? . . . To do justly, which means to issue a verdict, whether it is favorable or unfavorable . . . [in a derisive voice] 'Bishop, the Bible says judge ye not so that you don't be judged' . . .

22. Long, *It's Time*, 9.
23. Long, "Conquer and Subdue."

Your lifestyle and the way you walk should set judgment . . . Why do same sex [individuals] want to marry? Maybe it's because when they see the opposite sex marry, it looks like all of them are in hell . . . and they think, 'If God's way isn't working maybe we should try something else.' . . . We are judging unjustly because we are . . . hypocritical . . . What does he require of us: Live right as one to exercise judgment so that when folk behold the body of Christ . . . You now become the standard . . . The Lord said, I'm telling you about all of this power that you have but don't get arrogant . . . What we embark on Saturday . . . is a sign of unity and power of the people who have come to possess the kingdom.[24] [*Then Long invites the congregation to receive Holy Communion.*]

nder Submission paradigm uses a focus on church unity as a sign of God's activity in their midst. For Long, unity is a sign of power. Therefore, marching together "with one voice" serves a sign of the power of his ministry and of his ecclesiastical authority. Because Long moves through several unrelated topics, when he asks the congregation to speak with "one voice," it is unclear about which topic(s) they are expected to agree and to speak. In one example of a sermonic "rider bill," Long states,

God is saying that we [will] conquer and subdue . . . When you were born you accepted the mark of the beast which is the dollar . . . The financial system rules us . . . The reason Jesus and his disciples accomplished so much in three and a-half years is because they didn't go to seminary to try to figure God out . . . By now, you shouldn't be figuring out, 'Is that you, Lord?'[25]

Long does address social ills, the issue he most commonly examines is money. His apocalyptic reference to the "mark of the beast" associates financial systems with spiritual warfare between satanic and godly forces. In doing so, Long presents a theological interpretation of the financial system, but does not also explore the social and ethical issues associated with the financial system as part of a range of social concerns impacting blacks and others across the U.S. society.

ong, "Conquer and Subdue." In his entire sermon prior to the march opposing marriage equality, Long does not directly answer the question that he poses about why same-gender-loving people seek the right to marry other than to chastise his congregation for failing to set a higher moral example in their marital relationships as a possible reason why gay individuals seek the legal right to marry.

> When we walk on Saturday, we walk as a chosen generation . . .
> This is a royal processional of God . . . We proclaim the praises of
> Him who has called us out of darkness into the marvelous light . . .
> What does the Lord require? . . . To do justly, which means to issue
> a verdict, whether it is favorable or unfavorable . . . Your lifestyle
> and the way you walk should set judgment . . . Why do same sex
> [individuals] want to marry? Maybe because when they see op
> posite sex [individuals] marry, it looks like all of them are in hell
> . . . Your tail better rise up and do right.[26]

The main points of Long's sermons are often difficult to determine as
he commonly moves through various seemingly unrelated points without
providing any connective clues. Instead, he interweaves messages about is
sues that are highly popular and likely to excite his audiences, such as sex,
money and power. In the above sermon, for example, Long may inspire the
congregation by suggesting that they are God's chosen ones, whose proces
sion through the streets of Atlanta is a tacit demonstration of their praise
of God, and a proclamation that they have been chosen and redeemed by
God. To this inspiration, Long attaches a castigation of the congregation
for not living their lives in ways that serve as an incentive for gay people
to want to partner heterosexually. His criticism suggests that if his con
gregants were to set a particular moral standard by the way they live their
lives either gay people would not seek the civil right of marriage equality or
would be inspired to seek to be in heterosexual marriages. It is ambiguous
which of these potential goals Long is seeking.

Another key characteristic of spiritual authority as in
sion sermons is that preachers have the right, and perhaps even responsi
bility, to chastise congregations. The teaching is that for anyone to question
or not follow the leadership of preachers ultimately yields punitive conse
quences, and these consequences are sent by God to help ensure the unity of
the church. Long commonly interweaves chastisement with a forth-telling
of an unfolding movement of God.

> It is a year of judgment. The year of correction . . . This is not the
> year to worship in this house, and hate on your leader . . . You
> cannot sit up in the house of God and cause division, and think
> that God won't touch you . . . God will expose things, and tell you
> to choose . . . [if] you ain't right, you can't play when the L
> the house . . . God is preparing for his manifestation in his people
> . . . The greatest move of God right now is going on in the Middle

26. Long, "Conquer and Subdue."

ast . . . It is time for the body of Christ to rule and reign as he intended for us, and to be the head, and not the tail . . . God will promote some and demote others . . . God is making a shift . . . This is already happening . . . I don't want you to be confused and/or sidetracked. Hear me . . . Look at me . . . I am declaring this day by the power that God has given me as your pastor.[27]

ong utilizes chastising prophetic language to direct his hearers to use their spiritual authority in ways that he, as their priest-prophet, prescribes. McMickle argues that the priestly function of black churches "refers to their healing, comforting, and succoring work," while the prophetic function involves "its social justice and transforming aspects.'"[28] Because prophetic language, such as "God sent me here to tell you," is used, hearers are more likely to confer a high degree of authority to the preacher and to listen for a special transforming and empowering word from God, although social justice transformation may not be at the fore of what is preached.

s noted by Lincoln, tensions are likely between the charismatic authority of megachurch pastors and ecclesiastical authority of denominational hierarchies.[29] Although Under Submission sermons emphasize that honoring the authority of spiritual leaders is critical to the unity of the ong also contends that following the leadership of denominational heads blocks the movement of God. Long suggests that institutionally-granted authority is secondary to authority bestowed directly by God.

It is now time for the saints of God to rise up and possess the kingdom. We have substituted testimony for religious sayings . . . We have been corrupted by our religions and rules . . . Our appeal to the world is our testimony . . . Truth is what God says and religion is what men say God says. Many times we say things and put things on God that He just didn't say. And then we take what we say God said, and make it religious, then circle it with a denomination . . . And they make the gospel complicated . . . We call ourselves New Birth Missionary Baptist, but we ain't Baptist . . . We got to stop adding to the word of God . . . We need to know that we are saved by his blood . . . Our strength is in our testimony . . . And silence is impossible for the true believer.[30]

ong, "2006, the Year of the Man."

McMickle, *Where Have All the Prophets Gone?*, 17.

incoln and Mamiya, *Black Church in the African American Experience*, 388.

ong, "Power of Your Testimony."

Long and other post-modernist megachurches pastors express frus
trations about the ways in which their denominations maintain the status
quo and impede younger ministers from bringing new directions to their
denominations.

> Even the church has become stuck in rebellion by way of tradi
> tions, and we govern our rebellion by conventions . . . We have
> appointed people to make sure we don't grow . . . When God raises
> up another generation within the convention they're cast out be
> cause they won't stay within the order that they have elected folk
> to keep them in bondage.[31]

> God has not called us to maintain, God called us to reign . . . It is
> time for the saints of the Most High to stop looking for an event
> and be the event . . . We've got to reign in life by God.
> after me, 'Reign in life by one' . . . This is for the mature . . .
> comes from a foundation of power and authority . . . Apart from
> [God] we ain't doing nothing . . . Only those who are spiritual
> can discern this . . . [God] sent me here tonight to tell you . . . 'I'm
> doing a greater work in you.'[32]

As is the case for Jakes, there is a dialectic tension present in how
addresses the issue of authority. Long is unambiguous about the role of au
thority in conferring the "right to take what is yours," although he does not
explain how to ascertain "what is yours." He is incongruous, however, about
the source from which this right is conferred to him. On one hand,
claims that his authority does not come from institutions or institutional
leaders, but solely from God. On the other hand, based on the theology of
apostolic succession, he argues that in order to have authority, all people, in
cluding himself, must come under the authority of others placed over them.

## Hierarchized Preaching

While there may be a dialectic tension present in Under Submission with
regard to how ministers receive their authority, the message is unequivocal

---

31. Long, "Taking Authority of God's Word." Long's reference in this sermon to "con
ventions" reflects his unfavorable critique of the various black Baptist denominational
groups, including the National Baptist Convention U.S.A., Progressive National Baptist
Convention. See Lincoln and Mamiya, *Black Church in the African American Experience*
132–33 for a complete listing of the black Baptist conventions.

32. Long, "Reigning in True Authority."

that black Christians only receive their spiritual authority through their priest-preachers. The preachers, then, also have the authority to limit the scope of the spiritual and moral authority extended to the congregants.

ong, declaring that he has been sent by God with a specific message for the people, proclaims that only those who are spiritually mature can understand the full power and authority of God. Concomitant with such declarations is the claim that only those who submit themselves to his authority as spiritual leader can then access and utilize the power and authority of God.

nlike Don Saliers' argument that issues of power, class, and gender are generally "encoded" in sermons, these issues are overt in Under Submission model of preaching.[33] The themes of power and authority—spiritual, ecclesiastical, and political—are at the center of every sermon Long preaches. For Long, power is a resource which enables black Christians to "take" what he regards as "rightfully" theirs to have. This action of *taking* strongly denotes a process whereby individuals or a group might exercise their will over and against the resistance of others. The militaristic symbolisms, such as spear and shields appearing in the website of New Birth Missionary Baptist Church,[34] and language of conquering and subduing prevalent in Long's sermons, strongly reflect coercive uses of power—that is, taking even against the resistance of others.

In the Under Submission paradigm, sermons are socio-politically conservative and theologically constrictive. Although replete with messages about power, authority, and liberation, the type of authority and the process for liberation are narrowly directed and scripted by the preacher. The emphasis on hierarchized power relations and the focus on the empowerment of men are even more regressive than the messages about power in the broader U.S. society. Applying Cannon's test, Long's sermons participate in creating and sustaining socioethical values and sociopolitical practices that are oppressive to black churchgoers, especially women.

nder Submission paradigm does not reflect the purposes of black preaching suggested by Forbes to lift up a prophetic vision of justice for all people, inspire and empower black Christians to work as co-laborers with God to transform the world; and critique the culture in the ways it does or does not meet the needs of the global community.[35] In general, sermons in nder Submission model do not offer the kind of substantive liberation

Saliers, *Worship as Theology*, 140–41.

See the New Birth Missionary Baptist Church Web site: http://www.newbirth.org/.

Forbes interview by Cari Jackson.

for black Christians needed for this era. The narrow, virulent teaching to submit to spiritual leaders[36] or "suffer the consequences of being spiritually, financially, and morally bankrupt" impede the development and exercise of the moral authority of black Christians.

36. "Obey your leaders and submit to them, for they are keep watch over your souls and will give you an account. Let them do this with joy and not sighing, for that would be harmful to you" (Hebrews 13:17, NRSV).

# PART III

# Non-Coercive Coercion of the Black Pulpit

th year on I have increasingly regarded the church as an institution
which defended evils such as slavery, color caste, exploitation of labor and war.[1]

ECENTLY, I HAD A conversation with a young man who grew up in an
. church and shared with him my perspectives on the ethical implications emerging from aspects of traditional black preaching. He admitted
that he had never thought about pyramidal, power-*over* dynamics because
this way of relating in church was all he had ever known. As he reflected
on these implications, he asked the question, "What makes it difficult for
black Christians to recognize the oppressive dynamics and not work to
change them?" As I shared with him, the short answer is the curriculum
effect that normalizes coercive power relationships in subtle ways that are
deeply linked with the desires of black Christians to be in right relationship with God. The longer answer is that the curriculum effects of coercion
are expressed in three subtle ways that make it challenging for many black
churchgoers to identify the impediments and dis-empowerments to their
own spiritual and moral authority: (1) the indoctrination to link their trust
in and submission to God unequivocally with trust in and submission to
2) particular strategies used by some black preachers that perpetuate a long-standing pattern of preacher dominance as normative, and
) the complicity of some black churchgoers in coercing others to conform.

Du Bois, "Autobiography" in *Du Bois on Religion.* 7.

## In Pastor We Trust

Trust, a confidence in someone's words and actions as reliable and dependable often with minimal or no question or doubt, inspires black churchgoers to open themselves to be vulnerable in very intimate ways. Trust opens churchgoers to allow some black preachers to exercise power-subtle ways. Trust can be a non-coercive resource that opens the door for directing, controlling, or influencing of the actions of others, whether to their benefit or their harm. Where trust is strong "resistance" against the authority—institutional or charismatic—generally is not likely, nor is it needed.

Without trust, no matter how much authority is conferred upon black preachers nor how exceptional their charismatic gifts, the power of the pulpit is limited. But of course, the issue of pulpit power is not as simple as that. The challenge of trust is threefold. One, the role that black preachers and black churches have played in the lives of generations of black Christians as providing an ark of safety from the racial oppression in the broader society, black churchgoers are likely to allow themselves to be vulnerable at church. Two, to a large extent, the "curriculum effect" of black church culture and traditional black preaching socializes black churchgoers to trust their preachers without question. Three, even when some congregants begin to question what they see and hear from the pastors, others in the congregation, especially those in the upper levels of the church pyramid, often insist upon the allegiance to the pastor as a precondition for remaining in the community.

As Henry Mitchell and Richard Gula contend, for preaching ministry to be an effective resource for healing, uplift, and transformation, trust is critical. But what motivates congregants to continue extending unquestioned trust even when preachers' actions have breached their sacred trust, as in the cases of Henry Lyons and Eddie Long?

In his assessment of antebellum black churches, Du Bois argues that the long-term socialization of blacks during and post slavery greatly contributed to the creation of heightened vulnerability and trust in church environments, and to "the doctrines of passive submission."[2] H
because of this socialization effect, black congregants tend not only to trust their pastors, but also to acquiesce to their teaching and guidance. In such environments where trust is heightened to the degree of passive submission or acquiescence, resistance is generally not likely to be present.

2. Du Bois, "Souls of Black Folk" in *Writings*, 499.

Michel Foucault argues that notions of resistance or repression cannot fully explicate power relations. Going beyond notions of resistance, Foucault highlights "social contract" and "love-of-the-master" as two types of power relations that were present during 18th century relationships in
urope that might offer helpful insight for understanding the element of passive submission arguably reflected in historic and contemporary black clergy-congregant relationships.

Social contracts reflect the choices made by serfs to yield the power of their own "original right" of independent decision-making and free expression to their feudal lords.[3] They yielded this right for the purpose having a greater degree of safety that being under the protective arm of a sovereign nation could provide to them against the potential attacks from other groups. To strengthen their own safety, serfs supported the well-being of their feudal lords guided by the belief that if their lords were fiscally solvent and otherwise strong, the serfs would be guaranteed a greater degree of safety stemming from their connection with their lords.

In a way, this social contract is akin to the "trickle-down" economic theory espoused by some U.S. economists and elected officials for the past thirty years. The premise of the trickle down economic theory is that as those who are at the top of the economic pyramid are supported in making more money, they will be able to create jobs and otherwise stimulate the economy, which in turn, enables economic benefits to trickle down to the masses. Even though this theory has been shown not to be effective for fostering the financial health of the masses, there are many individuals within the masses who nonetheless advocate tenaciously for this approach convinced that it will eventually be to their benefit.

Similarly, many black churchgoers are convinced that their lives will be uplifted and experience greater safety and security as they extend uncompromising trust to their ministers. The social contract is grounded in the belief that well-being of their ministers will trickle down blessings into their lives.

In addition to the social contract relationship that emerged from a cost-benefit analysis aimed at heightening physical safety and economic security, Foucault contends that "love-of-the-master" relationships develop solely out of respect and love.[4] Love-of-the-master reflects the relationship between teacher and disciples, in which disciples willfully, without any negotiated contract, subjugate their opinions, values, property, and personal

Foucault, *Power/Knowledge*, 90ff., 138ff.
138ff.

rights to those of their master, in reliance on the presumed beneficence and greater wisdom of the master.[5] In this relationship, disciples operate with a belief that they honor their teachers' wisdom and beneficence by submitting themselves to their teachers. The presumption is that flowing from the wise beneficence of their teachers, the disciples will gain insight regarding how to navigate the various issues of life.[6]

Elements of both the social contract and love-of-the-master are present in varying degrees in contemporary black clergy-congregant relationships. For example, as illustrated when preachers invite congregants, including "television congregants," to "sow a seed"[7] into preachers' ministries. The theology of such invitations is that when a community of supporters provides financial support to the preacher and his ministry, by helping to expand the financial wealth of their favorite black preachers, those supporters will receive financial blessings as well. An example of love-of-the-master is a recently developed trend in some black denominational churches where congregants place money on the altar near the preacher while he is preaching; these funds are in addition to any tithing and other offering for the church that worshipers may give during the worship service, and are exclusively intended as thanksgiving to the preacher for the sermon.

Whether understood as a social contract and/or based on love-of-the-master, clergy-congregant relationships in black churches can set the stage for power imbalances regarding the relative exercise of moral authority of clergy and churchgoers, as well as for potential abuses of ministerial power. In both the social contract and love-of-the-master contexts, individuals

5. Ibid., 92.

6. While Foucault frames the love-of-the-master relationship as a type of non-coercive relationship in 18th century Europe, this style of relationship was classic throughout antiquity, and can be seen characteristic in the relationship between Jesus and his disciples.

7. It is a common practice at the end of most television broadcasts for preachers to invite their television viewers to "sow a seed"—that is, make a financial contribution to the ministry in order to help ensure the continued availability of those preachers' sermons on television. For example, much of the growth of Creflo Dollar Ministries/World Changers Church International (WCCI) has been its focus on ministry partners. "Creflo A. Dollar and Taffi L. Dollar . . . declare the blessing—the empowerment to prosper and excel—on our Vision Partners. Vision Partners of this ministry have a right to connect to the anointing that is on this ministry so that they, too, can prosper spiritually, socially, mentally, physically, emotionally and financially." See Creflo Dollar Ministries, "CDM Partnership," 2008.

8. This practice is especially observable in the Full Gospel Baptist Fellowship, Church of God in Christ, and some other Baptist and Pentecostal denominational groups, and more often offered to the bishops in those groups.

make choices to yield their human agency and moral authority to the direction of others (feudal lords and spiritual masters) based on the presumption that the quality of their lives will be better and that those to whom they yield their rights will honor the boundaries of their respective independence and authority. Foucault argues,

> the notion of repression is quite inadequate for capturing what is precisely the productive aspect of power . . . What makes power hold good, what makes it accepted, is simply the fact that it doesn't only weigh in on us as a force that says no, but it traverses and produces things, it induces pleasure, forms knowledge, and produces discourse.[9]

lthough the concept of repression does not embody power relations emerging from social contract or love-of-the-master, it does play a role in creating a black church culture in which individuals in the community are urged to repress their questions flowing from their own inner authority. A path is set that leads to ongoing struggle and submission.[10] One example of trust and acquiescence as a blend of social contract and love-of-the-master can be seen in "faith offerings" or "sacrifice offerings" that are common in many black churches. When pastors, or even guest preachers, want to raise a certain dollar amount in the offering, it is not uncommon for preachers to ask worshipers to form a line with offerings in their hands with a certain dollar amount to indicate their level of faith.

## Conflations and Inducements

Conflation and obfuscation of issues in preaching is comparable to the practice of "rider bill" voting in the legislative processes—that is, securing the passage of one proposed legislation by bundling it with key other legislative bills that are highly likely to be passed. Most often rider bills are attached to legislation that has high popularity among legislators and their constituents. When this practice is utilized in black sermons, the potential impact is a "whole-cloth" acceptance of ethical positions presented by

---

Foucault, *Power/Knowledge*, 119. Compare Foucault's argument with Bourdieu's contention that simply living and operating in a particular social field requires acceptance of and engagement in the rules of the social games, including the specific forms of social struggle and conflict that are norms in that social system. See Swartz, "Bridging the Study," 76.

Foucault, *Power/Knowledge*, 92.

preachers without critical reflection and examination of the various issues that are of ethical significance.

This pattern is most prevalent in the Under Submission approach, where issues related to individual financial advancement, abortion, marriage rights, and spiritual authority are blended without critical discussion.

The interweaving of such issues as sex, money and power are used as a maneuver to induce or seduce congregations whose life experiences have been shaped by socio-economic marginalization and oppression. This kind of maneuver reflects of rhetorical strategy that Brock describes as "symbolic inducements," used to garner an audience's cooperation and agreement with the speaker. As the Under Submission preaching model conflates and uses various symbolic inducements, and fosters the acceptance of moral issues that might not be at the forefront of congregants' concerns or have their initial support. Through the use of such symbolic inducements as money, prestige, power, and salvation, black congregants are often guided to endorse, and even promote, particular moral positions not based on their own critical examination, prayerful discernment, nor their own moral choice-making authority, but based solely on the preacher's positions on those moral issues.

The conflation of moral issues and the use of symbolic inducements as illustrated in the Under Submission approach best reflect what sociologist Dorothy Smith refers to as an "ideological rupture." Smith posits that the ways in which ideologies are organized and presented in public discourse insulates dominant ideologies from open and honest examination in relation to people's actual and historical experience.[11] An example of an ideological rupture occurs when Long links the economic conditions of his congregants with his moral stance on sexuality within the larger society.

Black Christians whose primary spiritual instruction is embedded with conflations and symbolic inducements may be less likely to challenge the power relations that privilege a few at the top of the hierarchy and marginalize the masses, whether within the black church or in the broader

If African American Christians have not experienced church as social environments that are safe for them to question and engage their own moral authority in dialogue with the status quo of power dynamics and the ethical implications of what is being taught, it is challenging for them to

11. Smith, *Conceptual Practices of Power*, 96. See Dino Felluga who argues that in effort to legitimize hegemonic forces, ideology "tends to obfuscate the violence and exploitation that often keep a disempowered group in its place . . . The obfuscation necessarily leads to logical contradictions in the dominant ideology." Felluga, "Modules on Marx: On Ideology."

recognize the elements of unjust systems and traditions within their black churches and the larger society and how to work toward dismantling them.

## Conformity, Compliance and Graceful Coercion

Du Bois contends that what may appear to be non-coercive social conditioning may often be a forceful transmission of ideas, beliefs, values, and traditions that steer individuals and groups toward specific sets of beliefs and behaviors. Du Bois asserts that blacks "are conditioned and their actions are forced not simply by their physical environment [but also by] the social environment of ideas and customs, laws and ideals."[12]

Guided by preachers, the social environment of black churches determine the parameters for "acceptable" beliefs and behaviors with which black Christians are expected to comply within their black churches or while operating in the broader U.S. society. While shared beliefs, norms, and customs are essential to cultural and group identity formation and to individual and group survival, when they function as preconditions for inclusion in a group, a foundation is laid for the potential disempowerment of individual social agency and moral authority. The sense of obligation to comply with the ideas, beliefs, and ideologies engendered through black preaching not only leads black churchgoers to likely complacency, but also can constrict what they perceive as a possible range of options for their lives. This obligation is especially seen in the Jakes' Economy of Power and nder Submission approaches. For example, Long urges,

> If you never learn the lesson of authority and submission . . . [D]isobedience opens us up to the devil . . . taking . . . your marriage, your finances . . . The whole corporate body has to be in order. So you need to minister to your friend next to you.[13]

Statements of this sort suggest two messages that foster the conformity of black worshipers: one, everyone in the congregation has to align in obedience to the leader or there will be adverse consequences for everyone in the church community, including those who are obedient; and two, each person in the congregation has a right/responsibility to challenge others to conform.

"In effect," social theorist Patrick Colm Hogan posits, "dominant ideology always has the first word, and so establishes the basis for other

Du Bois, "Dusk of Dawn" in *Writings* 652.
ong, "Taking Authority of God's Word."

opinions."[14] By embracing the values, interests, perspectives promoted in sermons, individuals are invited sub-consciously to substitute their own ideas, opinions, and desires for the ideologies that are preached, even if op pressive to them. A dominant ideology is conveyed through sermons with words like Jakes' "I refuse to pastor a people who do not think . . . Success is intentional. Nobody succeeds by accident."[15]

For Du Bois, the social pressure to conform to and comply with community norms has the same force, if not greater, than written law or physical threat. Hogan posits that often what may appear to be consensual choice-making and action emerges from an "informal coercion." explains informal coercion in this way,

> The diffuse danger of critical scrutiny from one's immediate so ciety is less intense than threats from the police or the fear of ter rorism, yet in many ways it is more pervasive. Indeed, perhaps the most routine or habitual form of coercion is not a matter of overt violence, or any punitive action, but rather the largely silent disap proval and withdrawal of one's peers.[16]

Hogan posits that neighbors, family members, and colleagues are in sistent upon the conformity of others for three primary reasons: ( of threats waged against the group unless all group members conform; ( nonconformity increases the likelihood of challenges to the moral legiti macy of the group's actions; and (3) nonconformity invites higher a degree of scrutiny of all of the group's actions if any individuals are not regarded as operating within the normative and acceptable range of behaviors. reasons appeal on the basis of an inner longing for individual and group survival. For black Christians who live with the reality of being excluded from the mainstream of the broader culture in many ways, the need to feel included and accepted within their black church communities not only

14. Hogan, *Culture of Conformism*, 78.

15. Jakes, "Position Yourself to Prosper."

16. Hogan, *Culture of Conformism*, 29. Wartenburg outlines three types of power- over: force, coercion, and influence. *Force* is the act of physically constraining a so cial agent from pursuing her desires or wishes. *Coercion* gears individuals toward a particular set of actions by altering a person or group's perceivable course of actions by presenting the possible consequences that are sufficiently undesirable. present when power agents fulfill their interests by misrepresenting their power over other social agents, who make choices different from what they otherwise would base on a belief in the misrepresentation as truth. Wartenburg, *Forms of Power*

17. Hogan, *Culture of Conformism*, 32.

provides a sense of safety and security, but is tantamount to life itself. For this reason, many black Christians, especially those who are gay, quietly endure messages that wound and re-wound them every worship Sunday so that they can remain a part of the community that is their home and their life. To gain social acceptance and avoid close social scrutiny, black churchgoers are likely to acquiesce to the normative beliefs and behaviors preached about from the pulpit.

ogan argues that informal coercion creates social environments in which individuals conform to group expectations and norms to avoid "the physical, economic, or emotional harm" likely if they question or challenge the status quo[18] or fail to achieve specific desired objects and goals.[19] The choices to conform are based on specific beliefs individuals may have about the options they perceive are available to assist them toward the achievement of their goals.[20] After engaging in a cost-benefit analysis of the key elements of a situation, Hogan suggests that often conformity is essentially a yielding to "the lesser of two evils."

Dorothy Smith contends that certain images, ideas, and information held by individuals are suppressed and replaced with universalized presentations of the issues in ways that the expression of divergent perspectives and experiences becomes highly unlikely.[21] Universalized definitions and explanations of life experiences then manufacture artificial forms of consciousness and knowledge about individuals' lived experiences that eclipse naturally occurring diverse perspectives and knowledge about life. When preachers proclaim that God always moves in one way in the lives of everyone who is without sin in their lives and yielded to God's sovereignty, congregants become inclined to trust this instruction even if does not line

ogan refers to this conscious avoidance strategy as "rational acquiescence."

"Calculated consent" is a conscious affirmative choice. Ibid.

To explicate calculated acquiescence, Hogan borrows from psychologist Jacques acan's delineation of three types of human goals: need, desire, and demand. Hogan defines needs as "goods, services, living conditions, and so on, the absence of which has a systematically and continuously deleterious effect on the physical or emotional health of people thus deprived Desires,' [he maintains are] "goods, services, conditions, and the like, the acquisition of which will, one imagines, bring pleasure (or relief from unpleasure), but which have no necessary, particular role in emotional or physical health." ogan explains "demands" as external expectations independent of genuine individual need or desire. Most "needs," Hogan contends, are generated by a particular social system itself then internalized by individuals within that system. Ibid., 40–41.

Smith, *Writing the Social*, 195.

up with their own experiences. After following the instruction of their preachers, if the quality of their lives does not improve, black churchgoers are likely to presume that it is caused by their limited faith or sin in their lives. For example, Jakes proclaims,

> You have the right to choose how you live the life that God has given you. It's an important choice, and you have to choose to live it God's way, or you'll get in the way of the destiny that God has for you.

With this teaching, the kinds of questions that ordinarily would naturally occur in response to the ideologies and worldviews presented in sermons are less likely to develop in black churchgoers. When divergent thinking does emerge, after engaging a cost-benefit analysis of the possible consequences of questioning the status quo message, individuals may often self-monitor and choose not to express divergent opinion or beliefs. When different perspectives are voiced, some black church communities insist upon members' conformity with what is preached. Moreover, when criticisms are voiced against the ideologies promulgated in sermons, individuals may be rebuked for rebelling against God.[23]

Smith contends that the process by which possible challenges are overshadowed includes: 1) certain segments of the protest are emphasized, largely out of context, and others are completely discarded, 2 assertions are extracted, conflated, and/or reassembled, and uni-dimensional definitions are employed, 3) attacks are made against the reputations of protestors, 4) events are exaggerated for rhetorical value, and 5) diverse experiences and perspectives are transmuted to specific identifiable and isolatable incidences as a ploy to cover the lack of credible evidence.[24] For example,

> This is a movement. It is a sign of unity and power of the people who have now come to possess the kingdom . . . How can two walk together unless they be agreed? If we ain't met, eyeball to eyeball, we can't walk together. If you ain't in agreement with this in heart and in

---

22. Jakes, "Leading Lady."

23. Collins contends that a specific "Curriculum" promoting one particular version of the truth as the only, ideal, or superior version often best serves the interests of elite groups or elites within a group. This expression of truth, Collins argues, is promulgated through exclusionary practices such as racial segregation and preferential gender roles. Whether or not motivated by a goal to serve the interests of elites within the black church community, black churches often promote one notion of truth and employ exclusionary/ preferential practices relating to gender and class. Collins, *Fighting Words*

24. Smith, *Writing the Social*, 218.

spirit, ah, ain't nothing. In a moment, we are going to take the Lord's Supper together because that's going to say that we are one.[25]

This particular excerpt[26] of Long's sermon illustrates all five elements of Smith's argument about how possible challenges can be overshadowed and leave little opportunity for anyone who wants to remain a part of that church community to question or challenge his authority as preacher or his moral positions. Throughout this sermon, Long anticipates possible challenges or questions that his audience may have, and then addresses those questions by conflating and reassembling his argument. For example, at the close of his sermon prior to the marriage amendment march, Long has the entire church community to share in Holy Communion; this act serves to overshadow any questions and washes any potential protests in the sacral "blood of the Lamb" at the Communion table.

By sharing in the Communion sacrament, worshipers are ritualistically coerced into tacit agreement with the preacher's worldviews for the sake of unity and in obedience to God. The Communion is designed to serve as a covenant that the congregation makes with God relating to marriage. This congregational act reflects an acquiescence that Hogan contends is a conscious[27] decision of individuals not to question or rebel against the dominant ideologies being presented in order to avoid the threat of harm. In the black church context, the kind of harm generally present would be the emotional harm of being castigated for disobedience and rebellion against God, for questioning the direction of the pastor is considered tantamount to rebelling against God.

---

ong, "Conquer and Subdue."

It must be noted here that while close to one dozen of Long's sermons have been included in this analysis, his sermon, "Subdue and Conquer," preached a few days prior to the procession through Atlanta to define marriage as between one man and one woman has offered more text than any of Long's others sermons or those of Jakes and Taylor useful for exploring the ways in which sermons can be used to constrict the moral authority of black congregants.

Wartenburg contends that for human agency to be truly consensual it must be conscious, and that often consciousness is not present in power relations. Wartenburg concurs with Steven Lukes' argument that in some contexts individuals over whom power has been exercised are not even aware that such has occurred, and as such may take actions that appear to be their independent, consensual choices yet in actuality are not. Bachrach and Barantz note that at times the non-decisions, inactions, as well as continued non-conscious actions of human agents might represent the effects of power having been exercised over them. See Wartenburg, 57.

Hogan argues that once people have organized their lives around achieving those goals allowable by the society, two things occur: one, they become endorsers of the system when they yield to the expected practice; and two, they actively begin to internalize a desire for the perpetuation of the system to which they have complied.[28] When this occurs, some individuals also become more likely to demand the conformity of others.

The Economy of Power approach illustrates how classifications based on spiritual maturity can be used to foster conformity. For example, a common theme Jakes expresses is, "This is a message not just for churchgoers, for those anointed by Christ,"[29] helps establish a superior class of Christians to which many aspire. The underlying message suggested is that any inclination to question, reject, or rebel against the preached message is a reflection of individuals' spiritual immaturity. Those who do not want to be perceived as spiritually immature are not likely to express concerns or questions about what is preached.

## A Politic of Domination

A form of social control and informal coercion suggested by Patricia Collins is "the politic of domination." Collins argues that "the politic of domination" functions by seducing, pressuring, or forcing individuals, especially those of subordinated groups, to replace individual and group needs, desires, and ways of knowing with the prevailing "specialized thought" of the dominant group.[30] For example, the Under Submission approach uses threatening language like,

28. Hogan, *Culture of Conformism*, 45.

29. Jakes, "10 Commandments of Working in a Hostile Environment."

30. Collins, "Matrix of Domination," 620. An example of a "specialized thought" common in black churches that has been promoted by the dominant group of male clergy and embraced lay women is belief that female ministers are to be regarded as subordinate to male ministers. Delores Williams contends, "The African–American denominational churches' sin against women exists partly because none of them has engaged a task much needed for the freedom struggle of black people, female and male . . . [N]o American denomination has seriously examined its doctrinal beliefs to discover whether they support racial, sexual, and class oppression." Williams, *Sisters in the Wilderness* 215–16. Also see Lincoln and Mamiya, who posit, "[W]omen are far more likely than men to move to second or third lateral appointments [regarding congregational size] than truly promotive stations. Few women are chosen for the large established churches of the central city, or posh, prestigious suburban churches." Lincoln and Mamiya, *Church in the African American Experience*, 298–99.

God is about to show up in a way that I cannot even tell you . . . But he's only going to show up in those, that remnant, who were willing to make the tough decisions . . . I ain't trying to scare you [but] God said, 'If you fight me, I'll deal with you.'[31]

Christian ethicist Mary Elizabeth Hobgood contends that institutions are used "to socialize people into 'proper' dominant and subordinate class, race, and sex/gender identities and roles" and that these identities and roles ultimately influence what individuals "think and value, how they act, and the degree to which they feel entitled to the benefits of society or blame themselves for disproportionately bearing its burdens."[32] By directing black Christians into expected dominant and subordinate roles, they are likely to adopt the kinds of thinking, knowing, and valuing that are consistent with their roles. This is what Delores Williams refers to as "control without coercion."

Thomas Wartenburg contends that although both dominant and subordinate social agents have the power of their human agency within specific socio-historical contexts, what determines who the dominant agent is and who the subordinate is each agent's interpretation and assessment of her or his own situation within the context of their social field.[33] In black church contexts, how preachers and congregants assess their respective ability or right to exercise their authority is shaped not only by the direct relationships between clergy and congregants but also the history of such relationships as part of the overall social field of black churches. This is further solidified by the roles that various church boards—such as deacons, ushers, trustees, missionaries, and church mothers.

Weber discusses the concepts of "honor" and "prestige" as inducements for coercing others to conform. When these inducements are present, whether formally or informally, by position on church boards or in other ways, churchmembers are likely to coerce others who have less prestige or honor. Weber contends,

> The power of political structures has a specific internal dynamic.
> n the basis of this power, the members may pretend to [have] a special 'prestige' and their pretensions may influence the external conduct of the power structure The realm of 'honor' which is comparable to the 'status order' within a social structure, pertains

ong, "2006, the Year of the Man."

obgood, *Dismantling Privilege*, 5.

Wartenburg, *Forms of Power*, 83–84.

also to the interrelations of political structure. Feudal lords, like modern officers and bureaucrats, are the natural and primary ex ponents of this desire for power-oriented prestige for one's own political structure. Power for their political community means power for themselves, as well as prestige based on this power.

Weber's analysis points to the value of feudal-like, hierarchical systems in providing honor, status, and prestige to the preacher-leaders who sit at the top of the hierarchy. As Weber's contention suggests, when the entire community is regarded as powerful and prestigious, the more powerful the preacher is regarded. His emphasis on being at the top of the hierarchical clergy-congregant pyramid reflects an oppressiveness characteristic of ministerial imperialism.

Therefore, it is not black preaching alone that contributes to the social conditioning or informal coercion of black congregants by black male preachers to defer their authority to that of their preachers. Fel low congregants also insist upon conformity and deference to preachers. Additionally, the social environment and governance practices, formed throughout the years of the structural developments of black churches, contribute to the maintenance of the status quo ways of relating. These are what Wartenburg refers to as the pre-behavioral and non-behavioral elements in a social field that establish the parameters for contextual ized knowledge, values and behaviors. Because of the history of power relations in black denominational churches, both charismatic preach ers (dominant social agents) as well as congregants (subordinate social agents) often may operate in their churches without any intentional or conscious strategy to constrain others, and nonetheless, directly and indi rectly participate in the constraint, domination, and oppression.

As the black church context has functioned traditionally, it greatly constrains the development of the kind of critical and independent

34. Weber, *Essays in Sociology*, 159–60.

35. In the late 1990s, I observed a complete shift in a group of black South when one white South African entered a room. Several very powerful and articulate blacks suddenly became disempowered and silent. The stark contrast in the behaviors, conversa tion, and overall carriage of the blacks I witnessed was intense. I observed no overt or in tended behavior on the part of the white woman to control, and later the blacks confirmed that there was nothing that she had done or implied, rather they were responding to their lived experiences and the history of their society. Having witnessed this in South helped me to recognize similar occurrences in the U.S. where such shifts are often more subtle, not only for some blacks relating with whites, but also blacks with other blacks, women with men, etc. based on power differentials implied in particular social fields.

thinking that blacks need to experience liberation in this century. Trickle-down blessings, love-of-the-master, and coercion to conform suffocate the capacity of black Christians to participate in social transformation for themselves and others. Unless these cultural norms are acknowledged, challenged, and interrupted, the present social, economic, educational, and spiritual realities of blacks today will continue to decline. The next chapter explores are range of ethical implications in the lives of black Christians and the broader black community emerging from the influences of contemporary black preaching and the coercive environment that some preaching fosters.

# 9

## Ethical Implications of Preacher Power

The paths and the higher places [of ecclesiastical leadership] are choked with
pretentious, ill-trained men and in far too many cases with men dishonest
and otherwise immoral. Such men make the walk of upright and business like
candidates for power too extremely difficult. They put an undue premium upon
finesse and personal influence . . . There are among them hustling businessmen,
eloquent talkers, suave companions and hale fellows.[1]

IT IS SURREAL TO read Du Bois' analysis written more than
about the tendency of black preachers to use their authority, charisma,
and trust to operate as "candidates of power." For, in light of the kinds
of stories in recent news headlines, this analysis could have been made
today. Du Bois' assessment not only highlights the tendency of black
preachers to dominate, but also points to the tendency black churchgoers
to allow themselves to be dominated.

The implications of this power-over dynamic are present not only in
black churches, but in all aspects of the lives of black folks.
erman states, "In exploring the intersection of race and religion, Du Bois
reminds us that religious life is never a realm unto itself but is always and
everywhere interwoven within the given social and cultural forces with
which it finds itself inevitably enmeshed."[2] Because of this enmeshment of
church life with personal life with public life, the curriculum effect of what

1. Du Bois, "The Negro Church" in *Du Bois on Religion*, 45.
2. See Du Bois, *Du Bois on Religion*, 57.

is preached in black church "doesn't stay in church," but shows up in all aspects of black folks' lives.

To look at the socioethical implications of the curriculum effect of and the coercive environment fostered by of black preaching, I return to my earlier definition of "social agency" as "the cognitive and emotional ability of individuals to make independent ethical, moral, and political choices and actions as members of a group or society." Understood in this way, social agency reflects a *power-to* accomplish intended goals, indeterminate of whether or not *power-over* others is exercised. Social agency is activated to the extent that individuals recognize their own divinely conferred moral authority and acknowledge the rights, privileges and responsibilities that come with that authority. Finally, social agency is guided by and representative of each individual's socioethical values and worldviews.

In the preceding chapters, I identified three major models of common themes in black preaching relating to power, social agency, and moral au-
conomy of Power (Jakes), Community Empowerment (McKen-
nder Submission (Long). These preaching models center around four key themes: who has authority, how it is attained, its purposes, and the impact authority has on the lives of those who use it.

This chapter investigates the potential implications of these themes in shaping the socioethical values and worldviews of black churchgoers. For socioethical values and worldviews play a critical role in determining how black Christians exercise their social agency within black churches and in the public sphere. As I look at the ethical implications of what is preached,
atie Cannon suggests, I will examine whose primary interests are served by particular constructions of meanings (including values and worldviews) and what kind of world is envisioned by those who have a major influence in constructing those particular meanings.[3]

## In Whose Authority?

ne of the most central features of the Christian message is that the power of God is available to be at work in the lives of individuals who align themselves with God. Jesus says to his ragtag-band of disciples, who are convinced that he alone has the power of God within, that they have the ability and the authority to do greater works than he did.[4] There is no sug-

121.

14:12.

gestion that some disciples have access to more of God's power based on status, position or length of time they had been disciples, nor that any have more authority to use that power than others. To the contrary, each time disciples vie for a closer seat to Jesus "when he comes into his kingdom," he tells them various parables to highlight the equality and justice in God. For Jesus, the only keys to accessing spiritual power and authority of the kind demonstrated as he performed miracles, spoke prophetic messages, and connected with people across diverse cultures, classes and life circum stances were prayer and fasting.

The tradition of apostolic succession, however, has corrupted the message of Jesus into a pastor-centered message of unequal and pyramidal access to the power of God. This religious tradition, in tandem with the cul tural role of black preachers that developed during the formation of black denominations in slavery, has yielded a highly preacher-centered model of how authority is attained that is prevalent in black preaching.

The distinctive messages about how authority is attained in each of the three paradigms of black preaching reflect specific understandings of power that have been shaped not only by the tradition of apostolic succession but also by a social environment in which racist and misogynistic oppression are normative. Given these influences, if preachers do not bring their own critical thinking to how their own socioethical values have been influenced, they are likely to perpetuate what has been handed down to them.

Both Economy of Power and Under Submission reflect a dualistic tension between power and authority attained directly from God and authority mediated through preachers. Under Submission even more strongly conveys the message that authority passes through the pastor only as congregants submit to the pastor. In contrast, Community ment facilitates black Christians in recognizing and accessing their divinely bestowed authority directly from God rather than pastors or any others.

Long's Under Submission presents dichotomous perspectives about the source of authority—on one hand, contending that authority comes only through submission to the resurrection power of Jesus Christ and is distinctive from institutional hierarchies; and on the other hand, holding tenaciously to an ecclesiastically-based chain of authority.
sion-style preaching utilizes this understanding of apostolic succession to establish an almost exclusively pastor-centered authority to set the moral direction of the community. Moreover, the Under Submission model de clares that adverse consequences are likely if congregants do not submit to

the preacher's authority. Sermons preached using the Under Submission model focus extensively on humanity as sinful, unworthy and spiritually According to this paradigm, black Christians should not to trust their own moral judgment but instead rely upon and defer to the moral authority of their preachers.

sing a Economy of Power approach, Jakes claims an authority from God that is largely pyramidal and trickle-down—that is, God gives charismatic gifts and authority to the preacher, who in turn, uses that authority to prescribe to the congregation formulas for life emulating his spiritual and material success. The Economy of Power-style preaching offers a more subtle approach than Under Submission to influence black churchgoers to submit to the authority of their preachers, conform to the preacher's socioethical values, and comply with the theoethical practices within their black churches. "I will not pastor" individuals "who do not think" strategically and intentionally in order to succeed reflects "symbolic inducement," a rhetorical maneuver to influence audiences to agree with the speaker unquestioningly. This use of the preacher's spiritual authority conveys to black worshipers the notion that if they do not adopt and adhere to all that the preacher teaches, they will not be able to access the healing, liberation, and abundance God has available for their lives.

The Community Empowerment approach defines spiritual and moral authority as given by God to congregations on the whole to participate in healing, repentance and social action for the common good of the community, nation, and world. Within this approach, the preacher's specific function is to inspire and challenge the church community to employ its God-given authority and responsibility to help heal and transform the world. The most prevalent message in the Community Empowerment preaching model is that God's power and authority are available to every human being, even without a preacher-mediator, because any mediation needed was already done on the cross of Jesus Christ. Community Empowerment declares that conventional assumptions about how power and authority are attained become turned upside-down through the work of Jesus. According to this preaching model, no one has to wait or submit to "those in authority" or "those who have charge over you" in order to have the authority of God, but rather to be in right relationship directly with God.

The curriculum effect of the messages in black preaching about how spiritual authority is attained has critical ethical implications. Sermonic messages that position black preachers as the mediators of God's power and authority infantilize the ethical decision-making of black churchgoers and perpetuate a preacher-centered culture that is marked by over-importance and lack of accountability. The emphasis on submission to the spiritual and moral authority of the pastor with its trickle-down theology of authority further disempowers black church folks in exercising their own moral au thority and over-privilege black preachers in using theirs. This system of pastor-centered authority has six potential adverse consequences on the socioethical and sociopolitical lives of black Christians.

First, built on the assumptions that the preacher has greater access to the voice of God, black churchgoers tend to rely more heavily on the moral direction from their pastors and under-utilize their own social agency and moral compass. When opportunities are not fostered for black churchgoers to develop and finetune their own ability to be guided directly by their own inner moral authority, black Christians become less equipped to differenti ate their own moral values and views from those of their pastors. Black churchgoers experience a high degree of spiritual and ethical dissonance, believing that what their own spiritual authority is telling them must be wrong if it is not aligned with the teaching of their pastors. Black Chris tians, thus, become locked into accepting what they are taught motivated by their sincere desire to be "in the will of God."

Second, black Christians are less likely to develop a critical ethical ear as they receive spiritual and moral instruction from their pastors. Black preaching that proclaims "what thus saith the Lord" may often be interpreted uncritically as if only representing "a word from the Lord" and excluding any personal biases shaped by the preachers' own values and worldviews. Black churchgoers may tend to be less likely to bring a critical ethical ear to information received from other authoritative voices in the public square. The emphasis on the role of preachers as the definitive proclaimers of God's word leaves worshipers less equipped to use their own spiritual and moral authority to discern and analyze socioethical and sociopolitical issues for themselves. When sermons are merely *received* instead of ethically black churchgoers are less adept at using their spiritual authority to make the scriptural text applicable in holistic ways for their own life circumstances.

Third, sermons that claim preacher-mediated authority provide lim ited options for black Christians to explore alternative perspectives for understanding the nexus of the scriptural texts and their own lived experi ences. When less likely to embrace their own God-given authority and to trust the still, small voice within as God speaks to them, black Christians become more likely to conform to the dictates of those in positions of authority and power even outside of their church contexts.

Fourth, when church environments present preacher-mediated authority as the only way for there to be unity, black Christians are less able to distinguish unity from conformity and less likely discover the richness of human community that holds both unity and diversity. As a result, black Christians are more likely to impose their religious views on others, even regarding issues of civil liberties for all people. Because of the narrow understanding of unity in community, black Christians are often less effective in being fellow citizens who respect the sociopolitical experiences of others in a pluralistic society.

Fifth, instead of directly addressing ethical and moral issues when presented, black churchgoers are more likely to exhibit behaviors that are unproductive, or even counter-productive, relative to their life goals and their intended witness to the love, grace, and power of God. Such behaviors might include constant complaining, passive-aggressive activities (such as working more slowly, taking excessively long lunch breaks, stealing office supplies from their workplaces), and projecting their frustrations onto their spouses, their children, or even strangers.

Sixth, pastor-mediated authority results in a tendency for black Christians to "worship" charismatic preachers as "demi-gods" and to not hold them accountable for their moral choices and actions. When black churchgoers are taught to rely on the moral direction of their leaders—who "have an inside track with God"—even when the still small voice within urges black churchgoers to question what they observe, many are not likely to hold their pastors accountable, but instead to acquiesce, be silent, and coerce others to into silence. Instead of holding their leaders accountable, black Christians are often only likely to say, "Let's just pray."

Seventh, trickle-down authority establishes a pyramid-based oppressive and marginalizing system of authority, rights, privileges, and blessings. Trickle-down authority promotes a culture of insiders and outsiders, with results comparable to the system of Apartheid. Those who are perceived as closest to the flow of authority, rights, privileges, and blessings become so focused on safeguarding their status in order to attain more than others— favor from their pastors, prestige, advance information about the ministry plans—that they consciously or unconsciously perpetuate a system of marginalization. Additionally, to protect their special status, those in the second tier of the church pyramid are not likely to challenge or hold their pastoral leaders accountable, but instead to deny, rationalize, minimize, or overlook their pastors' sexual indiscretions, questionable financial deal ings, and other breaches of ministerial ethics.

Eighth, pastor-mediated, trickle-down authority also fosters adverse consequences for the ethical lives of black preachers. When the power and authority of black preachers goes unchecked and unchallenged the tradition of preachers having power-over congregants perpetuates the unhealthy be lief among black preachers that spiritual leadership brings with it the right to command unquestioned authority. In church contexts where preachers are not questioned, almost inevitably abuses of ministerial power happen, such as those seen in the cases of Henry Lyons, Eddie Long, and countless others. For this reason, pastor-mediated, trickle-down authority ultimately does not serve the highest moral good for black preachers. Pastor-centered authority makes it more likely for black preachers to live with a sense of entitlement in ways similar to what many blacks criticize about the white hegemony of the broader culture. Additionally, the normative culture of preacher-mediated authority perpetuates the impact of double-conscious ness within black preachers and does not allow the healing that is needed for their souls and the souls of other black men and women.

The worldview that suggests that authority comes through and is to be sanctioned by pastors over-privileges black preachers and contributes to a kind of ethical unhealthiness comparable to that observable in results of over-privilege in U.S. whites. Preacher-mediated and trickle-down author ity set the stage for ministerial imperialism.

## The Role of Suffering in Authority

In the previous section, my discussion of who has authority naturally in cluded a look at how authority is attained. This section explores a very spe cific theme in black preaching relating to the attainment of authority—that is, the relationship between authority and suffering.

Each of the three paradigms of black preaching espouses a theology of suffering. All three preachers examined here indicate a strong identifica tion with of suffering in the lives of Jesus and others. How each preach ing model relates authority with suffering, however, is critically different. Whether suffering is regarded as bringing redemption, reward, or renewal impacts whether it is understood as a necessary experience for attaining authority or as an opportunity for greater insight for how to use God-given

How black Christians understand the role of suffering is critical to how they relate with and respond to oppression and other social ills. For this reason, the theology of suffering has profoundly ethical implications.

Traditionally, black preaching has espoused a theology of suffering that emerges from a blend of the Christian atonement theory of salvation[5] and from socio-theological attempts to explicate the insidiousness of anti-black genocide and oppression. This theology has brought both a sense of comfort and hope and a tendency to acquiesce to injustice and oppression.

conomy of Power approach proffers an understanding of suffering as redemptive—that is, a vital link the attainment of both salvation and authority. Yet the theme of redemptive suffering common to Economy of Power approach also reflects a critical dualistic tension. For example, on one hand, Jakes declares to black Christians that they must implore God to "rebuke [them] with all long suffering" in order for them to receive God's anointing and blessing upon their lives. "Many times God will put you in a situation that is not comfortable so that He might fulfill His purpose."[6] The theology of redemptive suffering conveys that God has a specific plan and design for each person's life, and as Jakes claims, "if you line yourself up with the script that God has for you no weapon formed against you shall be able to prosper." One the other hand, Jakes also chastises black Christians for remaining in poverty because to do so suggests that they have defined themselves by that condition.

s a result of this dualistic approach to redemptive suffering strongly Economy of Power, this theology fosters an ambiguous self-esteem and an ambiguous ethic in black Christians. It does not offer strategies for how to distinguish suffering that is sent by God, and therefore to be endured, from that which is brought by human hands, and thus to be disrupted. But instead shapes a worldview that interprets suffering, at both the personal and community levels, as part of the "plan of God" to bring

---

tonement is considered "the reconciliation of sinners with God especially through [the act of] the cross, as communicated through the gospels and sacraments. The cross is proclaimed as somehow resolving the human predicament"—that is, the sin of disobeying God as seen in Adam and Eve in the Garden of Eden runs through all humanity. The three traditional theories of atonement proffered by medieval theologians: 1) ransom ugustine), debt and reparation (Anselm), and moral influence and exemplar belard) contend that through the life, suffering and resurrection of Jesus Christ this human predicament is resolved. See Musser and Price, *New Handbook of Christian* , 42–43. Also see Hodgson and King, *Christian Theology*, 230ff.

Jakes, "10 Commandments of Working in a Hostile Environment."

them into greater spiritual maturity and closer to the abundance God may have designed for them.

While growing numbers of contemporary black preachers are promoting prosperity and abundance as part of God's plan, this attention is given primarily to ways of overcoming financially-related personal suffering, not to the identification of strategies for addressing the systemic issues that contribute to the suffering of masses of people. Cone argues, "the Christian affirmation of God's overcoming of evil in Jesus' cross and resurrection is not a substitute for making a political commitment on behalf of the liberation of the poor."[7] That is, much of the moral responsibility of Christians, outlined in biblical texts, calls for engagement in not merely extending charity to the poor, but participating in their liberation from poverty. While it can be argued that teaching and empowering individual black churchgoers how to advance economically is an individual-based form of liberation from poverty, this strategy alone does not accomplish the full work of liberation. By not also reforming the systems that create and perpetuate poverty, this approach has limited effect on masses of poor individuals, across social groups and generations.

Even more focused on suffering as redemptive, in the sion approach, Long proclaims, "Your trip to hell was to give you authority.[8] The theology of redemptive suffering is reinforced by sermons that emphasize the punitive consequences of not being in right alignment with God's plan for one's life. The Under Submission approach stresses the teaching that disobedience to God and those to whom God has given authority over others leads to "chaos and confusion" and to a punitive consequence of God's unresponsiveness to their prayers, from which the experience of suffering may ensue. For Long, suffering is both the path to authority and the consequence of disobedience. Similar to Economy of Power, it is unclear in this preaching model how churchgoers are to discern what suffering is signaling in their lives in given situations.

In comparison, according to the Community Empowerment model, God does not *send* suffering to individuals' lives but when life circumstances bring it, God *uses* suffering to help Christians to grow in their spiritual authority. For example, McKenzie urges black Christians to move beyond defining themselves based on their personal wounding and re-appropriate those wounds as signs of life and victory. "If Jesus got up from his wounds

7. Cone, *For My People*, 188.
8. Long, "Our Dominion."

so shall we." In this way, wounds are not to be understood as essential to attaining salvation or authority. It is not that suffering happens *upon* individuals who have no agency, but rather that individuals engage with suffering as agents with the authority to appropriate their experience in ways that bless their lives and the lives of others, as modeled in the life of Jesus.

The messages conveyed about the relationship between authority and suffering impact the socioethical lives of black Christians in three ways. First, the dialectic tension about the role of suffering makes it challenging for black churchgoers to discern whether or not they should acquiesce to suffering as God's redemptive pruning or transform the suffering experience to an expression of God's victory. Womanist theologian Delores Williams contends that the atonement theory supports violence, victimization, and undeserved suffering.[9] What Williams points to is a moral dilemma for black people whose socio-historical experience has been filled with marginalization and oppression. The dilemma is this: if suffering is redemptive, how do black Christians, especially given the socio-historical experience of merica, become equipped to use their human agency and moral authority when they are encouraged by sermons to acquiescence to and endure suffering? How are they to determine which social hardships they are divinely called to endure and which to transform? Instead of contributing to liberation, a theology of suffering as commonly used in black preaching contributes to a social conditioning of black Christians to accept and acquiesce to oppressive power relations they may experience within black denominational churches or in the broader U.S. society.

Second, the theology of redemptive suffering deters critical examination of the nexus of systemic social ills and individual lived experiences. nlike the suffering narratives of biblical Israel that focused on collective suffering, in today's era, the theology of redemptive suffering focuses almost exclusively on individual experience. As a result, the curative focus is on individual spiritual salvation, individual authority, and individual material advancement. The potential of these individual gains has been used as the symbolic inducements. And those potential blessings also serve as the incentives for black churchgoers to conform to the teachings of their pastors in order to avoid suffering. Additionally, these individualistically-focused curative measures and avoidance strategies for suffering greatly impede black Christians from looking critically beyond the immediacy of

Williams, *Sisters in the Wilderness*, 161ff.

their own circumstances and recognizing the socio-economic and political patterns of injustice impacting their lives and the lives of masses of others.

Third, the dialectic tension regarding the condition of human nature makes it challenging for black churchgoers to trust in the still small voice that they may hear within their own hearts and minds about their socio ethical choices. Whether sermons characterize humanity as innately sinful, immoral, and depraved or focus on humans as the *imago Dei* image and likeness of God"[10] greatly contribute to establishing the param eters for who has the primary authority for directing the moral choices of black Christians— preachers or congregants themselves.

Ironically, in sermons where sinfulness and depravity are the primary focus, somehow, the preachers often treat it as if they are exempt from this human condition. Black congregants have been instructed through the curriculum of black preaching to regard preachers as more spiritually and morally evolved and mature. In their spiritual earnestness, black Christians are more inclined to see fault within themselves easily, yet find it hard to recognize error in their preachers. This tendency greatly impacts how black churchgoers perceive their capacities for exercising their own social agency and moral authority. As perceive themselves as innately sinful and needing to suffer in order to "reign," black churchgoers are not likely to be actively engaged in efforts to transform oppressive systems and reform social con ditions for themselves or others. Additionally, they are less likely to hold accountable those who they regard as above them.

## The American Dream and Social Reform

I have explored the issue of who has the capability of accessing authority from God and how that authority is attained. In this section, I examine the scope and purposes of that divine authority. At issue is the question: What do black churches in the twenty-first century regard as their mission? Is their calling primarily to enhance the quality of life for black churchgoers as its sole focus, or to inspire and equip black churchgoers to participate as co-laborers with God in fostering the justice and liberation for all people?

Preaching within both the Economy of Power and Under Submission approaches urges black worshipers to use their spiritual authority to pursue and achieve the "American Dream." The cultural ideal of the " Dream" is the notion that in the U.S., if individuals work hard using their

10. Genesis 1:26–27, NRSV.

talents and skills they can achieve economic success. Conversely, the belief is that those in poverty and other life challenging conditions are largely, if not entirely, responsible for their circumstances.

In this era, increasing numbers of black preachers[11] are relating to issues of poverty in this nation of great wealth as individual suffering, and have developed prosperity techniques to assist individuals in getting out of the suffering of poverty. Little attention has been given to collective uses of spiritual and moral authority to address the systemic causes of poverty.

mong the black preaching approaches, Jakes' Economy of Power approach most strongly promulgates a worldview that blends the commonly merican ideals of "rugged individualism" and "manifest destiny" and fosters a theo-economics that focuses almost exclusively on individual spiritual and economic growth as predestined by God. Blending spiritual empowerment and rugged individualism, Jakes directs congregants toward the embrace of a world vision in which economic advancement is sought individualistically. Jakes proclaims, "You have to get engaged and you have to do something in order to win."[12] The Economy of Power approach proclaims that all individuals have a divine purpose and destiny for their lives that determine the parameters of their success. This approach also chastises people for living far below what is possible for them because they are not strategic enough in pursuing their destinies and are locked into perceptions of themselves shaped by their adversity.

Jakes argues, "People will not give themselves permission to prosper because they are accustomed to seeing themselves as poor."[13] Further, Jakes declares that many people are poor because they have accepted their poverty as an unalterable circumstance. This general assessment minimizes the impact of the systemic social factors that contribute to poverty, and casts most, if not all, responsibility for the economic realities in peoples' lives upon them. Jakes maintains, "The challenge is when you have defined yourself . . . through a codependent relationship or a simple thing like poverty."[14] This characterization of poverty as something "simple" overlooks the multivalent socio-historical economic factors that contribute to poverty. In the 1970s, Du

See Marvin McMickle who argues, that "patriot preachers" limit their messages to the issues of sexuality and abortion, and prosperity preachers limit their agenda to a "single focus on the personal gain of individual believers." McMickle, *Where Have All the Prophets Gone?*, 118.

Jakes, "Battle."

Jakes, "Frustration of Liberation."

Bois critiques black churches for catering more to those who had more finan
cial means and in a sense sacrificing the needs of those with limited income.

The rugged individualist pursuit of the American Dream uses a spiri
tual individualism for individual achievement and success. Because per
sonal responsibility is central in the Economy of Power approach, minimal
attention is given to mutual responsibility or to individual and collective
action for social justice. The Economy of Power perspective is what Chris
tian social ethicist Darryl Trimiew refers to as an "economic rights" ap
proach, which Trimiew contends not only fails to address the social causes
of poverty but also which ultimately helps "powerful economic elites to
retain power without explanation or accounting."[16]

Although Long also emphasizes individual material advancement,
he acknowledges the impact of what he refers to as the "kings of financial
systems" in shaping the economic realities of people's lives. The
Submission model recognizes the social systems that contribute to the
financial and other realities of life for blacks and others, systems that are
designed to disadvantage and disempower them. Long states, "When you
were born, you accepted the mark of the beast which is the dollar . . . But
God says your money is not supposed to work for the system, your money
is supposed to work for you."[17]

Similar to Jakes, Long castigates those who do "delay" in seizing op
portunities to use their spiritual authority to take back the economic power
that "the kings of financial system" have stolen from them. While
Under Submission approach does occasionally address systemic economic
issues, it does so with an emphasis on individually-based strategies for
navigating the marginalizing effects of the economic system, but does not
include a call to collective action for transforming that system.

Economy of Power and Under Submission preaching paradigms both
point attention to personal sin as a primary impediment impacting the rel
ative degree of success, wealth, and health of individual worshipers or the
congregation. Long declares, "If you follow along, there will not be a spirit
of poverty in this church And [if] you ain't right, you can't play when the
Lord is in the house."[18] Long makes a correlation between disobedience on
the part of individuals and "a spirit of poverty" for the church community.

---

15. Du Bois, *Du Bois on Religion*, 245, citing Du Bois, *The Crisis Writings*

16. Trimiew, *God Bless the Child That's Got Its Own*, 313.

17. Long, "Conquer and Subdue."

18. Long, "2006, the Year of the Man."

Long presents a communal approach to pursuing the American Dream that is framed by a congregant-to-congregant relationship that goes beyond mutual responsibility to guilt, and perhaps coercion.

In an effort to detract from indictments made against megachurches for their focus on economic prosperity, Long addresses the issue of individualism in this way,

> We've grown and changed the gospel of the kingdom to a selfish, give me, it's about me kind of thing. And nobody's reaching out to help one another. And all we're doing is trying to chase one another down to see who's doing what wrong so that I can have something on you.[19]

Beyond this form of chastisement, Long generally does not address collaborative social action that breaks from the pattern of self-interest and competition that may be concomitant with individualistic pursuits of the merican Dream.

With prominent attention given to empowerment for personal advancement and gain in Economy of Power and Under Submission, marginal attention is given to equipping black Christians to exercise mutual responsibility and compassion. Limited focus is given to what Du Bois urges is the charge of black ministers to be "active agents of social and moral reforms in their communities" in order to address systemic social justice isather, much of the focus reproduces the prevailing American Dream messages in the broader society promoting personal advancement within hierarchized power systems.

In contrast, the Community Empowerment approach does not convey messages promoting the individualistic aspects of the American Dream, but instead emphasizes a call to social justice activism to improve the quality of life for all people. Addressing the self-interested focus that McKenzie observes growing within black churches, she urges, "If your first concern is to look after yourself, you're going to lose yourself and you'll never find yourself." The Community Empowerment preaching model regards individual skills, abilities, and successes as assets from God to be used for the upbuilding of the community.

ecognizing the norm within the U.S. "American Dream" culture to villainize marginalized and oppressed individuals and groups, McKenzie challenges black Christians to make a decision "between blaming a victim

ong, "Taking Authority of God's Word."

and blaming a pattern of structural violence." The challenge issued by the Community Empowerment approach is to make ethical decisions that run counter to the cultural norms, just as Jesus did. As co-laborers with God, each person has the authority of God to make ethical decisions impacting not only their individual lives but also to help heal and transform the society.

The distinctions in the three preaching approaches to the Dream signal what Cannon contends are sermonic representations of how preachers envision the world. The messages conveyed in the sermons re lating economic and material gain fundamentally reflect their respective worldviews about moral authority. These respective worldviews influence the socioethical values and practices of black Christians in four ways.

First, the theology that promotes spiritual authority as a tool for achiev ing the American Dream both conflates individual and social realities and ignores the systems that contribute to individual life circumstances. For both the Economy of Power and Under Submission approaches to issues such as poverty and racism is to regard them as adverse life circumstances that can be overcome by individuals who have the fortitude to use their God-given spiritual power and authority to "pull themselves up by their bootstraps." Such a focus sets the stage for a lack of connection between the issues in people's individual lives and the social justice issues in the larger society, and an overall lack of focus on the community's participation in the healing, repair, and transformation of society.

With the "every-man-for-himself" perspective of the Dream, contemporary black preaching, as illustrated in Long and Jake's ap proaches, does not foster a critical examination of systemic social margin alization and how it directly manifests in individual lives. Without this kind of examination, black Christians may be more inclined to focus theologi cally and socially almost exclusively and narcissistically on their individual experiences and less likely to view themselves as spiritually and morally responsible for helping to reform adverse social systems that impact the society, and therefore, less likely to utilize their moral authority to address those systems. Additionally, black churchgoers are less likely to challenge and hold accountable the sociopolitical systems that perpetuate poverty and other forms of social oppression.

Second, the focus on the American Dream privileges economic pros perity as the definitive sign of God's blessing and regards it as the definitive barometer of "success" in accessing and using individual spiritual author ity. Because blacks have historically been politically and economically disenfranchised by racism, preaching that focuses on individual economic advancement likely appeals to the interests of black worshipers, as "having arrived" socially. This approach also greatly contributes to the shaping of a theo-economics that reflects a high degree of privatistic and individualistic use of authority—both spiritual and moral. Further, because aspects of the theo-economics within the Judeo-Christian scripture suggest that material wealth is a sign of God's favor,[20] black preachers regard this as a theological basis for an emphasis on what has come to be known in popular church culture as "prosperity preaching."[21]

The Black liberation theologian James Cone posits that the narrowly focused theo-economics commonly preached in black denominational churches emerges from particular perspectives about capitalism. According to Cone,

> The values of capitalism are so ingrained into American culture that many church persons assume that they are the same as Christian values . . . The belief that capitalism is Christian and Marxism is godless is one of the major reasons why the church has been a supporter of capital against labor, large corporations against small businesses, the rich against the poor.[22]

The focus on economic prosperity as a sign of God's favor continues to shape the socioethical values of black churchgoers to focus on economic wealth in the same way as the broader culture without any critique of the implications of those values on all people.

Third, as the Economy of Power and Under Submission approaches both regard wealth as a key indicator of spiritual favor and alignment with God, other ways that God's favor manifests in the lives of black churchgoers are tremendously devalued or even overlooked. Individuals may be experiencing amazing expressions of God's authority and favor, and not be able to recognize as such because it is not valued in sermons and in the church

---

Mitchem, *Name It and Claim It?*. Black preachers often cite the stories of Abraham, Job, Jabez, and the Hebrew people to underscore message that God expands the wealth of those who please God.

For example, much of the growth of Creflo Dollar Ministries/World Changers Church International (WCCI) has been its focus on ministry partners. "Creflo A. Dollar . . . Dollar declare the blessing—the empowerment to prosper and excel—on our Vision Partners. Vision Partners of this ministry have a right to connect to the anointing that is on this ministry so that they, too, can prosper spiritually, socially, mentally, physically, emotionally and financially." See Creflo Dollar Ministries, "CDM Partnership."

*For My People*, 184.

community. Individuals in the church may have incredible gifts and talents to share, not only for themselves, their loved ones, and church community, but with the world that may go unshared because they are under-valued.

Fourth, the focus on the American Dream as the barometer for spiri tual authority contributes to promoting a pattern of villainizing poor and working class people. It is normative in U.S. culture to blame people who are poor for their poverty, without knowing any of the circumstances sur rounding their lives and without holding the entire society accountable for the conditions that perpetuate systemic poverty. That is the easy way out, but not the ethical response to which the church is called.

Building upon Du Bois' argument that the primary role for black clergy is to teach morals, inspire Christians to live by the high ideals of Christianity, and serve as agents of social and moral reform,
that focus on the pursuit of the American Dream may likely strengthen the entrepreneurial savvy of some blacks, but grossly fails to strengthen and challenge the moral authority of most churchgoers.

The overall implications for preacher-mediated, trickle-down author ity, a theology of redemptive suffering, and a focus on pursuing the
can Dream greatly contribute to fostering a black church culture that is self-absorbed and narcissistic spiritually, socially, and economically.

23. Du Bois, "College-Bred Negroes" in *Writings*, 837–38.

# Toward a Critical Liberationist Ethic
# of Empowerment

[The black church] has accomplished much. It has instilled and conserved morals, it has helped family life, it has taught and developed ability and given the colored man his best business training.[1]

THE COLLECTIVE IMPACT OF black denominational churches upon black liberation has been characterized in divergent ways from affirming its effectiveness as a "healing catharsis," to challenging its contribution to the creation of "an ambiguous social ethic,"[2] to decrying its relative dormancy as an institution that has failed to foster liberation. Henry Mitchell claims that as a source of healing catharsis, black churches enable blacks to maintain their emotional balance and sanity amidst the socio-historical experiences of racial injustice in the larger white-dominated public

While Manning Marable argues that that black churches have failed to promote the liberation of black people.[4]

These divergent characterizations of black churches stem from three factors. First, these characterizations result from the tensions present between

Du Bois, *Crisis Writings*, 332.
    *Social Teaching of the Black Churches*, xiii.
Mitchell, *Black Preaching*, 111.
    incoln and Mamiya, *Black Church in the African American Experience*, 227, citing Marable, "The Ambiguous Politics of the Black Church," 211.

the espoused ideals and actual practice. According to Iris Marion Young, such tensions suggest that while the ideals are present in some form some of the claimed principles are violated.[5] Because of the relative theological and spiritual significance of these ideals, blacks continue to espouse them and experience the psychic dissonance when the ideals are not practiced.

Second, these divergent characterizations emerge from the double-consciousness in the collective psyche of black Americans. Because the re ality of double-consciousness is still largely ignored in black churches, little has been done to address it; instead, black preachers and other church lead ers continue to bring "mixed messages" about socioethical issues of power and community ideals of liberation as well as theological issues of salvation.

Third, these varied characterizations reflect the divergent expectations of the role that black churches are to play in the lives of black folks who seek to witness the power of the gospel of Christ. For some black preachers and black churchgoers, it is enough to have a sacred space of community that provides respite and healing from the realities of racial oppression. For some black Christians, it is enough to receive spiritual uplift through the dance, the music, and the preaching that helps us deal with the varieties of challenges in this life. For some, it is enough to be inspired by broader vi sions of what our lives could be, and receive spiritual, psychological, and fi nancial strategies to actualize those broader visions. Yet, for others, none of these visions of church is enough. For some of us, the witness of the power of the gospel of Christ is only fully expressed when the experience of black church includes the spiritual uplift, respite, life strategies, full inclusion and honoring of all people, and equipping worshippers to be co-laborers with God. This is a liberationist vision of church that sees black churches as environments where preaching equips black churchgoers to use their spiritual authority in tandem with individual and collective gifts and talents to promote liberation, justice and freedom for all people.

For black Christians—congregants and preachers alike—who long for the realization of this vision of church, I propose three critical liberationist strategies for black preaching: (1) recharacterization of the role of black preaching, (2) reconceptualization of power, and (3) remoralization of au thority. It is not enough to say that we are committed to the freedom and liberation of black people. We must also make critical changes in how we "do church" to make that freedom and liberation more possible.

5. Young, *Justice and the Politics of Difference*, 6–7.

## Recharacterization of the Role of Black Preaching

The realization of such a vision requires a break from learned submissiveness and a sense of second-class citizenship that are deeply intertwined in the collective black psyche. The realization of a liberationist vision of church requires honest acknowledgement of the hole burrowed into the collective souls of black folks by historic and continued racial oppression. This hole is reflected in the lives of many blacks as a need for constant affirmation, a presence of low self-esteem, envy of successes and accomplishments of others blacks, and so on. Black churches as training grounds for a liberationist ethic demands intentional focus be given to helping to heal the holes in our souls, including those within black preachers. Black preaching must work to disrupt historic and contemporary values, norms, and traditions within the black church that contribute to the perpetuation of disempowerment and oppression in any form.

Many black churchgoers derive a sense of higher social status from their positions in the church hierarchy. Furthermore, in many ways, black church culture rewards churchgoers for pressuring or coercing their peers, not to "rock the boat," but to accept and maintain church cultural norms as they are. Therefore, without direct messages in sermons, and other aspects of the worship and governance life of the church, intentionally designed to counter "non-coercive coercion," congregants are likely to continue perpetuating intragroup oppressions. To interrupt these potential patterns, preaching must be innovative regarding how it critiques and challenges informally coerced agreements to operate within normative social relations that are oppressive and regarding how it creates opportunities to dismantle those normative relations. Black preaching must be more definitive in identifying, critiquing, and transforming power imbalances in all social arenas, including within black churches. It must articulate a critical race liberationist ethic of social empowerment.

cross the generations of black churches, black preachers and congregants have made significant changes, many to which there was great initial resistance. Such changes have included: allowing women to serve in various missionaries and other lay leadership roles; adding piano, organ, drums, guitars as instrumentation in worship; ministers attending seminaries; including praise dancers in worship; women wearing pants, bright colors, or earrings to church; women becoming ordained as pastoral leaders; church members being urged to attend college; church members receiving financial advice at church; encouraging churchgoers to talk openly about life injuries; women being elected to ecclesiastical/ episcopal leadership; and so on. These changes have enhanced the quality of the lives of black churchgo ers and strengthened the effectiveness of black churches.

One of the aspects of black churches, however, that has remained greatly unchanged across those generations is the authoritarian, power-over leader ship style of black preachers. Cheryl Sanders queries "whether the eloquent, charismatic, authoritative preacher" leadership style is most effective in facil itating social empowerment.[6] Authoritative black preaching promotes defer ence to and conformity with the moral positions of black male preachers, thus, constrains the exercise of the moral agency and the development of the moral authority of black Christians. Sanders' query points to a critical need to examine the implications for the empowerment of blacks stemming from the correlation between certain approaches to power reflected in preaching and pastoral leadership styles.[7] For preaching, both in content and form, reflects and shapes pastoral leadership.

Just as black churches have been effective in making other changes across the centuries, it is critical to do so in the twenty-first century church, especially as it relates to the role of black preacher-pastors. Why? Because both what we preach and how we preach are impeding the full spiritual actualization and social liberation of black folks. What we are preaching and how we are "doing church" is resulting in generations of young black people not coming to church because they regard black churches as places of inhospitality, inauthenticity, and hypocrisy led by power-hungry preach ers and maintained by conformist church members.

The power-over dynamics observable in black churches contributes to the reasons offered by many black men who do not attend church. Given the social realities of the larger U.S. culture where black men (and women) are expected to be submissive, many refuse to come to church where the same insult to their personhood is happening as well. Because of the self-interested socialization now as common in black churches as in the larger

---

6. Sanders, *Worship as Theology*, 99.

7. Martha Long Ice delineates characteristics of modernist and post-modernist lead ership styles that may be useful for such an examination of the correlation of preaching and leadership approaches. Specifically, Ice suggests that a modernist orientation reflects such characteristics as hierarchical, authoritarian, exclusive, dualistic extrinsic authority, individualistic, and personal as private. Post-modernist includes egalitarian, democratic, inclusive, pluralistic, communal, intrinsic authority, and the personal as societal. Ice, *Worldviews*, 13.

society, black churches are giving less attention to addressing today's social ills than they have in past generations.

What, then, should be the role of and the message of black preaching for the twenty-first century? I begin with Du Bois. The vision of the role of black preachers, as suggested by Du Bois, is to enhance the lives of blacks ） teaching morals, 2) inspiring the high ideals of Christianity, and 3) serving as agents of social and moral reform.[8] Building upon Du Bois' contention, there are three key clarifications about the role of preaching that provide a critical framework. First, the understanding of "teaching morals" as used here is not suggestive that a singular voice should set the moral standard and moral path by which all others in the community are required

ather, teaching morals must be understood as assisting individuals in developing their own moral agency and their own inner moral compass. Second, "inspiring the ideals of Christianity" is to be understood as an invitation to conversations within church communities about what those ideals are. By engaging all members of the community as interpreters of biblical scripture, they become conversation partners who are more able to envision and live out those agreed Christian ideals in their present-day realities. Third, "serving as agents for social and moral reform," is not the sole role of the preachers, but the collective role of faith communities. As black preaching inspires churchgoers to engage in social reform, they become more able, individually and collectively, to use their moral agency in new and creative ways essential for this era.

Next, I return to the vision of black peaching offered by Dr. Jim Forbes. For Forbes, black preachers are members of the community, not elevated above the members, and who have the specific role in the community to preach prophetically the message of justice, hope, peace, and love for all people, as modeled by Jesus. Black preachers are also called to lead church communities in engaging a serious critique of the culture, and to care for the needs of the global community.

To function in these roles of black preaching outlined by Du Bois and Forbes becomes possible as black preachers shift from preacher-centered and trickle-down authority approaches and utilize dialogic preaching and hermeneutical honesty as resources for liberative preaching.

Du Bois, "College-Bred Negroes" in *Writings*, 837–38.

## Dialogic Preaching as Ethical Discourse

The predominate form of black preaching can be characterized as akin to the style of teaching that Brazilian educator Paulo Freire refers to as "banking" style pedagogy,[9] where concepts are deposited uni-directionally from authoritative teachers to passive students. Freire argues that dialogic learning experiences, where the pedagogical relationship is built on respect for the perspectives that students have to offer, are more productive than banking-style pedagogy. Dialogic processes facilitate more holistic learning for both students and teachers that is more meaningful and transformative for them as individuals and as members of a society.

Preaching that utilizes banking-style pedagogy is more likely to yield the kinds of ethical consequences such as limited critical discernment, not holding leaders accountable, narrow understandings of signs of God's favor, individuals not trusting in their own spiritual authority, conformity, compliance, informal coercion, and so on.

Greater social empowerment can be fostered, according to Freire, by a dialogic, liberative process. Freire suggests that engaging in a process of dialogic teaching can help students, and their teachers, to develop a greater critical awareness about social realities, and thus, become more able to perceive social, political, and economic contradictions that perpetuate social oppression.[10] With greater critical awareness of these contradictions both students and teachers are more equipped to take action against oppressions in whatever forms they manifest.

One characteristic feature of some black preaching, the call-and-response dialogically-styled preaching reflective of the West A
making tradition, offers an opportunities for dialogic innovation.
dialogic in form, call-and-response is, nonetheless, largely rooted in a banking approach. Traditional call-and-response does not facilitate substantive

---

9. Freire argues that banking style of pedagogy is characterized by several oppressive attitudes and practices: (1) teachers teach and students are taught; (
everything and students know nothing; (3) teacher think and students are thought about; (4) teachers talk boldly and students listen meekly; (5) teachers discipline and students are disciplined; (6) teachers choose for students, and students comply; (
students vicariously act through the actions of teachers; (8) teacher chooses the program content without any input from students, and students adapt to it; (9
the authority of knowledge with their own professional authority, which is then set in opposition to the freedom of students; and (10) teachers are the subject of the learning process, while students are mere objects. Freire, *Pedagogy of the Oppressed*

10. Ibid., 19.

conversation on ethical issues that includes the theoethical voices of the congregation. Call-and-response patterns, *directed* exclusively by preachers, often bring the expectation that worshipers should repeat and pattern their responses and their beliefs after those of their preachers almost by

ven worshiper-initiated responses such as, "You better preach," affirm what is preached and do not necessarily reflect or encourage black worshipers to engage in their own critical thinking and prayerful reflection.

Social ethicist Jürgen Habermas argues that "'communicative action,' the process of giving and criticizing reasons for holding or rejecting particular claims,"[11] is essential for creating social relations that support the kinds of conversations needed to ensure the freedom and equality to which all human beings have rights. Habermas contends that absent intentional communicative action, which enables critique and challenge of normative claims, free and uncoerced agreement is not likely.[12] In order for moral claims to have real validity, those who are affected by those claims need to be included in a legitimately conversational process.[13] Similarly, Traci West contends that U.S. Christians "are accustomed to monopolizing the discussion of public values" and that this monopolization impedes the kind of meaningful discourse needed for social justice.[14] West suggests that justice requires "more ethical communal relations," that is, social relations that do not reflect power-over, but the mutuality of power-to dynamics.

When preachers argue that their moral direction is guided by Christian scripture, they greatly overlook the influence of their own interpretive lenses that have been shaped by their own life experiences and worldviews. The widespread tendency within black churches to ignore these factors contributes to the pattern of relating to black preaching as if words spoken "out of the mouth of God." As West suggests, social justice cannot happen absent equitable exchange of moral opinions and mutual shaping of values among individuals and communities as they interpret their sacred texts together. Ethically-based dialogic preaching is critical to the building of "communicative action" and "more ethical communal relations" that in turn enable black churches to better equip black churchgoers for using their moral agency in the broader U.S. society.

Cavalier and Ess, "Political Computer."

abermas, "Justice and Solidarity."

abermas, *Moral Consciousness and Communicative Action*, 66. Also see Antje Gimmler, "Discourse Ethics of Jürgen Habermas."

*Disruptive Christian Ethics*, xv.

Just as trickle-down blessings alone are not likely to improve the quality of life for a whole community, as Habermas argues that strengthening individual freedom and moral agency alone does not foster liberation and justice. For true justice and liberation to be experienced in the community, there must be an intentional process of building solidarity.
reflects a concern for the well-being of other individuals within the community as well as the community on the whole.[16] A focus on solidarity moves individuals beyond their own self-interest to recognize and regard the needs of others as important as their own. This understanding of solidarity is framed in Christian scripture in this way, "Love your neighbor as yourself."

To strengthen preaching as a resource for socio-ethical empowerment, black preaching must consider incorporating diverse dialogic preaching methods that enable meaningful communicative action among churchgoers, such as:

1. Inviting churchgoers to respond, as part of the sermon, to critical moral questions presented in sermons and engaging in preacher-congregation dialogues,

2. Inviting lay members of the congregation to preach and co-preach at regular occasions throughout the course of a year to bring divergent voices, and

3. Offering small group discussions of sermons, not led by the preacher, to enable churchgoers more intimate space to share various perspectives and explore biblical texts.

Recognizing that these suggested alternatives do not fit within the performative preaching norms of many black churches, and that some churchgoers may be greatly disquieted and uncomfortable with such

15. Solidarity is a critical element in the ethic of discourse, which H in this way, "Under the pragmatic presuppositions of an inclusive and noncoercive rational discourse among free and equal participants, everyone is required to take the perspective of everyone else, and thus project herself into the understandings of self and world of all others; from this interlocking of perspectives there emerges an ideally extended we-perspective from which all can test in common whether they wish to make a controversial norm the basis of their shared practice; and this should include mutual criticism of the appropriateness of the languages in terms of which situations and needs are interpreted." Habermas, "Reconciliation through the Public Use of

16. One key biblical example of the invitation to solidarity is Jesus' urging to " the Lord your God [and] love your neighbor as yourself" (Matt 22:3–39).

dialogic methods, preachers, working collaboratively with Christian educators and lay leaders, would need to prepare their congregations. Essential to preparing churchgoers for this shift in preaching form is presenting the precedents for this dialogic process reflected in biblical texts—such as, the admonition of Jesus to his disciples, "greater works than these shall you do" ). Preparing congregants might also include inspiring them by preaching about the church as the place to build and practice greater socio-ethical empowerment needed to transform their lives and those of others.

In this way, the role of preachers is to use multiple sermonic and dialogic methods to facilitate the strengthening of individual moral agency and deepening of the relationships that individual churchgoers have with God. Preachers, in this sense, are not the moral compasses or arbiters of moral authority for individual black churchgoers, but *facilitators* and *role models* of individual and social transformation. Furthermore, by de-centering the banking approach of preaching, black preaching emphasizes its pastoral role to nurture and facilitate spiritual authority within black Christians.

## Hermeneutical Honesty

nother critical tool for transformative preaching is hermeneutical honesty, where preachers disclose to churchgoers the intersection of their personal lived experiences and their interpretation of scriptural texts. The foundation of hermeneutical honesty is a critical self-reflection process offered lizabeth Hobgood. "Critical self-consciousness" is vital to the creation of an ethical agenda that dismantles "the monopolization of social Critical self-reflection involves preachers and congregants alike taking responsibility for the beliefs that they often absorb from traditional banking-style preaching that contribute to reproducing and perpetuating marginalizing systems of social power.

During its institutionalization during the 3rd-4th centuries, Hobgood contends, "traditional Christian theology and ethics adopted the dualism and hierarchy of the Western philosophical worldview" that were consistent with the social values of the wider society.[18] Pyramidal clergy-congregant relationships, reflecting pastor-centered and trickle-down authority, lead contemporary black churchgoers to endorse the preachers' moral positions on a range of such socio-spiritual issues as money, women's health, homosexual-

obgood, *Dismantling Privilege*, 31–32.

29.

ity, education, criminal justice system, domestic violence, and so on without discussion, yet often with uncritical, over-simplistic and dualistic (treating all issues as black and white, and refusing to see the complexities of gray therein) approach. This uncritical approach both perpetuates hierarchical power-over relations within black churches and serves as the basis for assessing social and political leaders in the larger U.S. society.

Absent hermeneutical honesty, black preachers are less likely to rec ognize the interpretative aspect of their sermons that are shaped by an admixture of their life experiences, worldviews, and divine inspiration. common approach among black preachers is to deny the influences of their own life experiences in shaping their theology and to espouse the belief that all that they preach is divinely inspired, or even directed, by God. Hermeneutical honesty insists that black preachers recognize how the lived experiences of key actors in biblical stories shaped how they understood and interpreted God, and the choices they made. If black preachers were to apply this same hermeneutical honesty to themselves, they would rec ognize and preach about how their own life stories intersect with Christian scripture and shape their theological understandings. Flowing from this would come a richer personal identification with the biblical "heroes" and "sheroes" more possible for all black Christians. Identification with their struggles and victories, the strengths and weaknesses, and the ways that they doubted themselves and doubted God, together enables Christians to appropriate the text more fully for themselves.

Critical self-reflection is also essential to hermeneutical honesty be cause of the tendency of interpreters of scriptural and other texts to bring a presumption of comprehensiveness. To counter-balance this presumption, sociologist of religion Otto Maduro urges interpreters of texts to engage in a "conscious autocritical"[19] approach, because a truly comprehensive interpretation is unachievable. Engaging a conscious autocritical approach strengthens the overall effectiveness in informing and motivating audienc es, enables clearer understanding within the interpreters of own inquiry, and helps them focus the audience's attention more clearly on the most salient social issues and relationships.

19. In his examination of sociology of religion as undertaken in see Maduro, *Religion and Social Conflict*. Also Mark Taylor emphasizes the criticality of honesty about the impact of one's 'hermeneutical self-implicature.' That is, for Taylor, the theologian must bring self-awareness and honest disclosure about his or her social particularities and the ways in which these become interconnected with the cultural and political contexts being addressed. Taylor, *Remembering Esperanza*, 1–22.

s black preachers engage in a conscious autocritical approach to their sermons and do not hold themselves out as having the full and comprehensive divine truths for people's lives, they help foster the kind of relationships with God both for themselves and black churchgoers that more fully reflect the ongoing creative and revealing dimensions of God. Instead of relationships with God that are defined solely by obedience to a punitive God, a conscious autocritical approach to preaching facilitates relationships with God that are guided by God's love. This shift helps empower black churchgoers to identify and access their own spiritual and moral authority as they operate in the public sphere as collaborators with God.

Some black preachers might be concerned that to publicly acknowledge messages conveyed through their sermons as only their own interpretations of scripture and to invite congregants into conversation about the application of scripture to contemporary moral issues might lead to faith crises in the lives of some Christians or give justification to others to commit sin if they are not sufficiently constrained by religious prescriptions. Paradoxically, creating intentional space for honest dialogue among clergy colleagues and among clergy with their congregants about ethical interpretations and understandings of scripture strengthens the beliefs and moral authority of the whole community. The moral authority of individuals and the community are strengthened because of the difference between the curriculum effect of the uni-directional banking-approach to preaching and the dialogic communicative action of preaching that is rooted in a liberative process. This kind of communal reflection can help churchgoers strengthen their own spiritual connection as they engage their faith more critically and become more empowered in their own faith and moral journeys.

ermeneutical honesty expands the capacity for black sermons to be used as resources for strengthening the moral authority of worshipers by enabling black preachers to engage in critical dialogue with congregations about the complexities of the moral choices impacting congregants' personal lives, the church community, and the broader society. Hermeneutical honesty aids preachers and congregations to go beyond dualistic approaches to all issues as either individual *or* social and all behaviors as right

wrong, and to delve more deeply into the interconnections of individual and social and to identify moral principles and actions that help guide the social action needed to address the range of complex justice issues present in our contemporary social reality.

In addition to examining the impact of their own worldviews upon what they preach, black preachers must have the courage to examine the impact of the black preaching tradition itself in shaping their worldviews and what they preach. To foster greater empowerment and liberation of black Christians, black preachers must be willing to reflect honestly on how aspects of what has been handed down through the black preaching tradition that may have been useful as the moral compass for earlier periods in black church history may now impede how black Christians may need to function as moral agents in today's society. Because the social circumstances today are more diverse and complex, black preaching has a greater role in equipping black Christians in using their moral authority to navigate not only through anti-black racism, but also through a range of issues impacting their lives.

## Reconceptualization of Power

While various social institutions may propose to develop and strengthen ethical skills useful for individual empowerment and social transformation, Patricia Hill Collins argues that, they simultaneously require docility and passivity."[20] Thus, in order to establish processes of empowerment and transformation that are unencumbered by docility and passivity requires a "reconceptualization of power."[21]

Because of the socio-historical factors within black churches, including social norms and practices that may serve to reinforce a pattern of docility, the power exercised in black preaching must be reconceptualized in order to be used more intentionally and deliberately to break through marginalizing norms and practices and to foster greater empowerment of black Christians and their sociopolitical liberation. To accomplish this, there is a need for black preachers to lead the way via their preaching to help reconceptualize power itself.

In his last address as president of the Southern Christian Conference, Martin Luther King, Jr. defines power as

> the ability to achieve purpose. It is the strength required to bring about social, political, or economic change . . . [T]he concepts of love and power have usually been contrasted as opposites . . . What is needed is a realization that power without love is reckless and abusive, and love without power is sentimental and amnesiac. Power at

20. Collins, "Matrix of Domination," 620.

21. Ibid., 617.

its best is love implementing the demands of justice. Justice at its best is love correcting everything that stands against love.[22]

ing's argument that the ultimate aim of power must be to accomplish "the demands of justice" provides a needed reframe of power as a resource to be utilized for the empowerment and transformation of entire communities, not just for some individuals. As King contends, power, without love as its guide and social justice as its goal, gives rise to abuse.

Black preaching that is not rooted in the aims of justice results in a misdirection of the power of the pulpit. Because, as Du Bois suggests, black ministers are "candidates for power," black preaching must be consciously aimed at justice and consistently guided by love in order to avoid a propensity toward ministerial imperialism and abusiveness, a narrow focus on individual socioeconomic advancement, and the perpetuation of the uncritical acceptance and acquiescence to social injustice.

The constructs of power must be re-imagined from a trickle-down process to a process of equal access. Empowerment must be recast from a traditional uni-directional process whereby some individuals give authority to, liberate, or empower others to a bi-directional, dialogic process of engagement between individuals who bring diverse perspectives, life experiences, and social statuses that collectively foster communal liberation. Without an intentionally dialogic process where all parties are encouraged to and supported in utilizing their God-given authority, black churches continue to preserve a system that lends itself to privileging the authority of an elite group of "empowerers" over others.

mpowerment must be reconceptualized as more than a process of therapeutic release for blacks to cope with racism in the U.S. Black preaching must also be a medium for inspiring, challenging, and equipping black congregants to speak and act with individual and collective authority in ways that follow the demands of love and social justice. Black preaching has a responsibility to nurture blacks using their moral agency to question status quo power relations, challenge normative marginalizing traditions, and participate in interrupting unjust systems present within the black church as well as the broader society. The reconceptualization of power requires that black

ing, "Where Do We Go from Here: Chaos or Community?" in *Testament of* . According to psychiatrist Carl Jung, "The power-instinct wants the ego to be 'on top' under all circumstances, by fair means or foul." He continues, "Where love reigns, there is no will to power; and where the will to power is paramount, love is lacking. The one is the shadow of the other." Jung, "On the Psychology of the Unconscious," 38, 53 [P 50,78].

preaching be used intentionally as a resource to reframe the power relation ships between clergy and congregants from pyramidal to egalitarian, and thus, to model and practice what can be possible in the broader society.

Christian scripture is replete with stories of how Jesus both recon ceptualizes power and models for his disciples to use their own authority in doing the same. While it is common in traditional black preaching to highlight these stories, they have been reflected upon in ways that make Jesus' acts distinctive from what we as Christians are called to do. embracing of Jesus message "greater works than these shall you do," un encumbered by notions of preacher-sanctioned or trickle-down authority, prompts black preaching to acknowledge the authority of the Spirit that is available to each Christian to place the needs of the global community before maintenance of religious norms.

Biblical scholar Obery Hendricks offers a scripturally-based approach to how power and authority can be distributed and exercised in ways that integrate personal and social transformation. Hendricks asserts,

> Jesus was a political revolutionary . . . [T]he message he pro claimed not only called for change in individual hearts but also demanded sweeping and comprehensive change in the political, social, and economic structures in his setting in life . . . [The] goal of his ministry was to radically change the distribution of author ity and power, goods and resources, so all people . . . might have lives free of political repression, enforced hunger and poverty and undue insecurity . . . Jesus sought not only to heal people's pain but also inspire and empower people to remove the unjust social and political structures that . . . were the cause of their pain.[23]

Hendricks suggests that an integrated approach to addressing personal struggles and social injustices is central to the Christian message and val ues. While short-term solutions for individual lives may be possible without such integration, more long-term, sustainable interruption of sociopolitical and economic injustices is not possible without such integration. core of Jesus' message about how to affect and transform systemic social change is a call for a redistribution of authority and power.

Consistent with what Jesus teaches and models, black churches are called both to redistribute power and authority and to integrate reflec tions on personal lived experiences with critiques of social injustices. To facilitate a more equitable distribution of power and authority for blacks

23. Hendricks, *Politics of Jesus*, 5–6.

and other marginalized groups, black preaching must respect and engage the moral authority of black congregants. Sermons that respect, activate, and strengthen innate moral agency are essential to the task of social empowerment and liberation of blacks. Such sermons inspire and equip black Christians to use the power of their authority in the broader public sphere by establishing a standard for engaging in dialogues about justice and preparing them for bringing their voices to such dialogues. To maximize the effectiveness of social empowerment-oriented sermons, there is also a need for church norms and practices that foster the engagement of the moral authority of all black congregants, across gender, age, income, education, sexual orientation, and so on.

Jesus' nonconformist engagement with religious and social institutions and systems of his era is undergirded by a clear understanding that how power must be understood and exercised not only as a social and political reality, but also a spiritual condition. It is spiritual because it shapes people's understandings of their access to the power of God. For this reason, black preaching has the responsibility to strengthen the black church as an environment in which black folks gather not only to celebrate the Jesus who reconceptualizes power to do great works, but also equips black Christians to participate in the greater works of love, healing, and justice needed today.


## Remoralization of Authority

key dialectic tension impacting the moral authority of black Christians is a general tendency to regard *personal* transformation and *social* transformation as distinctive from one another. To address this dialectic tension, a third critical strategy needed realize a liberative vision for black preaching is the remoralization of authority. Remoralization of authority aids in strengthening black Christians' moral authority by harmonizing the polar tensions relating to power and authority that are present in some common approaches of black preaching. Remoralization is needed, according to Sanders, to facilitate a recalibration of what is understood as *personal* and in order for transformation on either level to be effective and sustain-bsent remoralization, individuals can be personally transformed

Sanders, *Empowerment Ethics for a Liberated People*, 105.

and yet remain socially disengaged, or personally unchanged even while being socially conscious.[25]

Sanders defines remoralization as a process that enables individual and communal strengthening in three ways: one, restoration of individuals and communities to "a morally sound condition;" two, development of the ingredients of "courage, discipline, and staying power" necessary for love and acceptance to be sustained; and three, "creative problem-solving through [the] restoration of mental clarity and order."[26] Although this definition of remoralization is problematic in that it presumptively suggests that all individuals and communities have at some prior time experienced a "morally sound condition" or a state of "mental clarity and order" to which they can be returned, it is useful in that it emphasizes the criticality of integrating personal and social transformation.

Building on Sanders, I define remoralization as an intentional process engaged in religious institutions, homes, and other ethics-shaping environments whereby, an integrated understanding of individual and social interests, rooted in respect for the innate moral agency within each human being, works to ensure the ongoing nurture of individual spiritual authority in order to foster practices that strengthen the capacity, commitment, and courage of individuals to make moral decisions guided by both the power of love and justice for all people, as modeled in Jesus Christ.

While this definition presupposes that an innate moral agency is divinely given to every human being, it does not presume that each person has lived in environments that have acknowledged the existence or nurtured the development of that agency. This definition of remoralization is intended to charge black clergy with the responsibility to assist black churchgoers in exploring how to use their individual moral agency and their spiritual authority in ways that transform their own individual lives as well as the society. This understanding of remoralization reflects a recognition that most moralizing influences, both within black churches and the wider U.S. society, are largely rooted in dualisms—such as, good/bad, us/them, black/white, Christian/non-Christian, clergy/laity, love/power, individual/communal, and personal/social—that offer only piecemeal attempts at liberation, transformation, and justice. To counter most moralizing influences in our society, remoralization of authority must be an ongoing process; it must be engaged in intentional ways each time the community

25. Ibid.
26. Ibid., 104–5.

of faith gathers. Remoralization is based in the premise that the justice, freedom, and liberty in God can only be fully experienced in the collective voices of the community, and that no one leader or group of leaders has all or knows all that is needed to bring about sociopolitical justice and liberation not merely as ideals but as social realities.

Collins contends that distinctive systems of injustice and oppression survive as interlocking parts of an overall system of domination, and therefore, in order to accomplish substantive social reform requires a rethinking about each system that fosters injustice.[27] Black churches, and the black preaching traditions within them, must reflect on ways that black churches, through the voice of black preaching are intricately interwoven in the fabric of domination of U.S. blacks, not because of any intention to do so, but because of oppressive practices that have been uncritically handed down and maintained. Now is the time for black churches to reimagine the role of black preaching needed for this era so that it more effectively interrupts oppressive systems rather than maintains them.

## Redefining Injustice

emoralizing authority requires a broader understanding of injustice and an expanded vision of justice. If black Christians only espouse the ideals of justice without also examining concrete ways that injustice may present by their own actions, they are more likely create a narrative that they are living the ideals that they espouse. It is only by having clear markers of injustice that black churchgoers and others can best reach toward those ideals.

s Iris Marion Young argues, to create greater possibilities of justice,[28] we must think outside of current notions of what is normative. It has commonly been normative for the black preaching curriculum to highlight injustices as various forms of oppression (economic, educational, practices in the justice system, employment, housing) meted out by the white hegemony upon blacks. Given the history of racist experiences that have been so prevalent in the U.S., it has been easy for black preaching to feature racism against blacks as *the* injustice. With an almost exclusive focus on race-based

Collins, "Matrix of Domination," 616.

Young defines justice as the degree to which a society contains and supports the institutional conditions necessary for the realization of values for the "good life." As well, she defines "injustice" as any institutional constraint on self-development or self-determination and institutional domination. Young, *Justice and the Politics of Difference*, 37ff.

injustices, however, it has been rare for black preachers to identify and challenge other forms of oppression, including those within the church. Not only are other forms of oppression largely overlooked in many black pulpits, they are even promoted, especially the denigration of poor people, marginalization of women, and vilification of gay and transgender persons.

In light of that social reality in black churches, womanists and femi nists have boldly sought to highlight and challenge patriarchal and misogy nistic injustices that have been part of the social fabric and moral thread of the black church throughout its history. As it is written in the "pages" of the Civil Rights movement, black women who championed the cause of making discrimination against women a part of the discussion about civil rights were told that *their* issue needed to wait until the race issue was addressed. Additionally, there are countless stories of black Christians excommunicated from their church pews and pulpits because their sexual ity is deemed to be an unembraceable aberration from, or perhaps attack against, God's plan for human expression. There is also a growing trend in black churches to regard those who are poor as completely responsible for their economic condition, and therefore unworthy of any assistance other than occasional beneficent handouts of food and clothing. Countless black churchgoers have experienced being devalued, disempowered, and discarded and not being seen in their dignity as human beings, as children of God. And yet these forms of mistreatment, by and large, have not been regarded by preachers and other church leaders as injustice. In some ways, women, poor people, and gay people experience greater levels of justice, love, and inclusion outside of black churches than within them. To move more fully toward a liberative vision of black churches in the twenty-first century demands a critical redefinition of injustice and oppression.

Young's definition of oppression as social power relations that foster exploitation, powerlessness, or cultural imperialism provides a useful start ing point for a redefinition of injustice. Ministerial imperialism lays the foundation for injustices within the black church that become so norma tive that they are not recognizable as unjust. Injustice may be difficult to recognize because most unjust structures, systems, practices, and values are the normative ways of living in community by which blacks and others are socialized to accept. Injustice is often so deeply intertwined with those things that people enjoy, their self-identity, or familiar aspects of their "cul tural home" that they may be slow to recognize, challenge, or participate in dismantling injustices, at times, even when impacting their own lives.

e-defining injustice must be guided by King's theory of justice as that which reflects an integration of power and love "correcting everything that stands against love." Building on King's theory of justice, I offer that *injustice* is the work of any structure, system, policy, norm, practice, or action that runs counter to and works against love and that devalues, denigrates, marginalizes, or exploits others.

endricks' characterization of justice is also useful to the enterprise of redefining injustice. Hendricks 'suggestion that justice begins with redistribution, or sharing, of authority and power, goods and resources to ensure that all people are free from oppression provides a useful starting point for reconceptualizing power and remoralizing authority to help identify the ways in which power dynamics in black churches foster injustices.

To use black preaching more fully to recognize injustice and work for justice is essential for the continued work of the sociopolitical liberation of blacks. It necessitates engaging a critical examination of the normative messages conveyed through black preaching to assess their implications for interrupting or perpetuating the bounds of injustices reflected in systems, structures, and traditions that devalue, denigrate, or marginalize others—whether in the black church or broader public sphere. Without a higher level of hermeneutical honesty within black church culture about the impacts of the double-consciousness based curriculum effect on black churchgoers, we cannot be fully free. What shall we say to these things?

# 11

## A Closing Word

The Negro minister needs to know and do more than merely preach and pray. They must be possessers of pubic spirit and have the capacity to cooperate in educational and other social movements.[1]

IT IS MY HOPE that the preceding chapters help black church folks to re flect more critically and honestly about the implications and impacts of what we preach and how we respond to what we hear preached in our churches. It is also my hope that if we say that our preaching and our overall witness is guided by the teachings of Jesus Christ, that we be hon est about what the ministry and mission of our churches really are.

The church's mission is known through its preaching. Throughout the history of black denominational churches, there have been tremendous so cial challenges to which churches have raised up and responded. We have new challenges in this era that require creative partnerships and collabora tions between those who are called to ordained ministry and those who are not. But we are all called to be ministers. Let us create ways that provide more nurture and more opportunities for all black Christians to bring their God-given talents and abilities as co-laborers with God.

Guided by the critical liberationist strategies, black churches have the potential to expand the twenty-first-century church mission to foster sus tainable social justice action that transforms individual lived experiences

1. Du Bois, "Negro Church," 194.

as well as broader social realities. Without intentional critical liberationist efforts to expand beyond approaches to black preaching that foster an imbalance in social power and moral authority, black preaching will continue to perpetuate hierarchical clergy–congregant relationships that ultimately impede social empowerment, liberation, and justice.

While the role of preaching in assisting worshipers to cope with and navigate through anti-black racism continues to be an important tool needed for social empowerment, this role alone is not enough. The greatest significance of contemporary black preaching lies in its potential to contribute to social reform, not only for blacks but for all people. Black preaching must especially foster social empowerment by strengthening the moral agency of blacks and building their collective moral authority. Black preaching must equip black Christians to identify the linkages between personal and social transformation in ways that inspire them to participate in transforming power systems that marginalize any people. Black preachers share the responsibility of leading the charge to engage in substantive social critique and modeling and inspiring their congregations to this level of critique.

I urge that preachers in black denominational churches come together to reimagine black preaching and pastoral leadership for the twenty-first century. I mean really think outside the historical boxes. First, such venues would provide the opportunity for black preachers to reflect on the perceived benefits and challenges of redistribution of power, remoralization of authority, redefinition of injustices. And to come together to wrestle with how to nurture the spiritual authority of black Christians in ways that strengthen the witness and ministry of black churches in addressing the contemporary issues impacting the daily lives of African Americans and others. In such forums, black preachers might grapple with several critical questions to be reflected in their sermons, such as:

> What might the spiritual leadership role of black pastors look like today that enables both the nurture of individual spiritual authority and church unity?
>
> What responsibilities do individuals share in seeking the liberation and justice for all people?
>
> In what ways are black Christians and church communities to be co-laborers with God in seeking justice in the twenty-first century?

4. How can we foster a perspective that seeks the integration of individual struggles and systemic injustices when our congregants are dealing with so many personal challenges that need to be overcome?

5. How do we help black church members know that participating in healing and transforming the world does not mean abandoning our focus on heaven?

Second, these venues could also be a therapeutic and renewing space specifically for black pastors in which they can talk about and release the stresses, fears, and challenges of the pastoral role in this era. This would be a safe, liminal space for black preachers. While there are many forums nationally in which black preachers gather, these settings are primarily to provide tools and strategies on church growth, church administration, and preaching. Without a venue in which to express their own life struggles, black preachers are less able to preach in ways that facilitate the liberative experiences needed in the lives of African American Christians.

Third, these forums could provide opportunities for intentional dialogue between black preachers and black religious scholars to honor the resources and mine the wealth of knowledge of these respective professional communities. The purpose of such dialogue is to engage in honest acknowledgement of the presence and impact of double-consciousness that is manifest in all aspects of African American experience, and to begin developing comprehensive strategies for addressing its impact.
the conversations would bring together some of the best strategies across academic disciplines to explore what kinds of leadership strategies can be most effective for fostering social liberation of blacks today.

For the healing of the souls of black folks.

# Bibliography

live News," Atlanta NBC-WXIA, February 3, 2011. Online: http://www.11alive.com/
news/local/story.aspx?storyid=176187&catid=40.

ghion, Philippe, and Patrick Bolton. "A Theory of Trickle-Down Growth and
Development." *Review of Economic Studies* 64.2 (1997) 151–72.

. *The Black Spiritual Movement: A Religious Response to Racism*. 2nd ed.
noxville: University of Tennessee Press, 2001.

Banjo Shelly. "Churches Find the End is Nigh," *Wall Street Journal*, January 25, 2011.
ccessed June 22, 2012, http://online.wsj.com/article/SB10001424052748704115 40
4576096151214141820.html?mod=WSJ_RealEstate_LeftTopNews.

eader Henry Lyons Faces Charges of Racketeering and Theft." *Jet*, March 16,
nline: http://www.highbeam.com/doc/1G1-21250129.html.

Barna Group. "Do Churches Contribute to Their Communities?" July 13, 2011. Online:
http://www.barna.org/congregations-articles/502-do-churches-contribute-to-their-
communities%202011%20Dec%205.

. Susan. *Contemporary African American Preaching: Diversity in Theory and Style.*
ouis: Chalice, 2003.

Bourdieu, Pierre. *Language and Symbolic Power.* Cambridge: Harvard University Press,

Brock, Bernard L., Robert L. Scott, and James W Chesebro, editors. *Methods of Rhetorical
Criticism: A Twentieth-Century Perspective.* Detroit: Wayne University Press, 1972,

Campenhausen, Hans von. *Ecclesiastical Authority and Spiritual Power in the Church of the
First Three Centuries.* Translated by J.A. Baker. Peabody: Hendrickson, 1997.

atie G. *Katie's Canon: Womanism and the Soul of the Black Community.* New
York: Continuum Publishing Co., 1995.

*Teaching Preaching: Isaac Rufus Clark and Black Sacred Rhetoric.* New York:
Continuum, 2002.

obert, and Charles Ess. "The Political Computer: Democracy, CMC, and
abermas." In *Philosophical Perspectives on Computer-Mediated Communication,*
edited by Charles Ess 197–230. Albany, NY: SUNY Press, 1996.

Coleman, Monica A. "Roundtable Discussion: Must I Be a Womanist?" *Journal of Feminist
Studies in Religion* 22.1 (2006) 107–13.

Collins, Patricia Hill. *Black Feminist Thought: Knowledge, Consciousness, and the Politics of
Empowerment.* 2nd ed. New York: Routledge, 2000.

————. "Black Feminist Thought in the Matrix of Domination." In *Social Theory: The Multicultural and Classic Readings*, edited by Charles Lemert, Westview, 1993.

————. *Fighting Words: Black Women and the Search for Justice.* Minneapolis: of Minnesota Press, 1998.

Cone, James H. *For My People: Black Theology and The Black Church* Orbis, 1984.

Craddock, Fred B. *Preaching.* Nashville: Abingdon, 1985.

Creflo Dollar Ministries. "CDM Partnership." 2008. Online: http://www.creflo dollarministries.org/About/Partnership.aspx.

Crocker, Lionel. *Rhetorical Analysis of Speeches.* Boston: Allyn & Bacon, 1967.

Doob, Leonard W. *Personality, Power, and Authority: A View from the Behavioral Sciences* Westport: Greenwood, 1983.

Douglass, Frederick. *Life and Times of Frederick Douglass.* Boston: DeWolfe & Fiske,

Driver, Tom F. *Liberating Ritual: Understanding the Transformative Power of Ritual* Boulder: Westview, 1998.

Du Bois, William Edward Burghardt (W. E. B.). *Against Racism: Unpublished Essays, Papers, Addresses, 1887–1961: W. E. B. Du Bois.* Edited by H Amherst: University of Massachusetts Press, 1985.

————. *The Crisis Writings.* Edited by Daniel Walden. Greenwich: Fawcett Publication, 1972.

————. *Du Bois on Religion.* Edited by Phil Zuckerman. Walnut Creek:

————, editor. "The Negro Church: Report of a Social Study Made under the Direction of Atlanta University." Delivered at Atlanta University, May 26, University of North Carolina at Chapel Hill, 2001. Online: http://docsouth.unc.edu/ church/negrochurch/dubois.html.

————. *Writings.* Compiled and annotated by Nathan Huggins. New York: The of America, 1986.

"The Eldad Medad Men's Ministry." St. Paul Community Baptist Church, Online: http://www.spcbc.com/eldadmedad.

Eyerman, Ron. *Cultural Trauma: Slavery and the Formation of African American Identity* Cambridge: Cambridge University Press, 2001.

Felluga, Dino Franco. "Modules on Marx: On Ideology." In "Introductory Guide to Critical Theory." Purdue University, November 28, 2003. Online: http://www.cla. purdue.edu/English/theory/marxism/modules/marxideology.html.

Forbes, James A. *The Holy Spirit and Preaching.* Nashville: Abingdon, 1989.

————. Interview by Cari Jackson, January 22, 2002.

————. *Whose Gospel: A Concise Guide to Progressive Protestantism.* New York: The New Press, 2010. Kindle Edition.

Fortune, Marie M. *Is Nothing Sacred?* New York: Harper & Row, 1989.

Foucault, Michel. *Power/Knowledge.* Translated and edited by Colin Gordon. New York: Pantheon, 1980.

Frazier, E. Franklin. *The Negro Church in America/The Black Church Since Frazier.* Sourcebooks in Negro History, edited by C. Eric Lincoln. New York: Schocken,

"Freedom Riders Documentary." Public Broadcasting Network, March http://video.answers.com/diane-nash-personality-based-leadership-517320004.

Freire, Paolo. *Pedagogy of the Oppressed.* New York: Continuum 1970.

Gebara, Ivone. *Longing for Running Water.* Minneapolis: Fortress, 1999.

ntje. "The Discourse Ethics of Jürgen Habermas." November 2003. Online: http://caae.phil.cmu.edu/cavalier/Forum/meta/background/agimmler.html.

Govier, Trudy. *Dilemmas of Trust*. Montreal: McGill-Queen's University Press, 1998.

ichard M. *Ethics in Pastoral Ministry*. Mahwah, NJ: Paulist, 1996.

abermas, Jürgen. "Reconciliation through the Public Use of Reason: Remarks on John awls's Political Liberalism." *Journal of Philosophy* 42.3 (1995) 117–18.

———. *Moral Consciousness and Communicative Action*. Cambridge: MIT Press, 1990.

———. "Justice and Solidarity: On the Discussion Concerning Stage 6." *Philosophical* 21.12 (Fall/Winter 1989) 32–52.

Henry. "Practicing Liberation in the Black Church." *Religion On-line*. June nline: http://www.religion-online.org/showarticle.asp?title=778.

*The Word Made Plain: The Power and Promise of Preaching*. Minneapolis: Fortress, 2004.

acewell, Melissa Victoria. *Barbershops, Bibles, and BET: Everyday Talk and Black Political Thought*. Princeton, NJ: Princeton University Press, 2004.

ayden, J. Carleton "Conversion and Control: Dilemma of Episcopalians in Providing Religious Instructions of Slave, Charleston, South Carolina, 1845-1860." *Historical Magazine of the Protestant Episcopal Church* 2 (June 1971).

bery M., Jr. *The Politics of Jesus*. New York: Doubleday, 2006.

iggenbotham, Evelyn Brooks. *Righteous Discontent: The Women's Movement in the Black Baptist Church 1880–1920*. Cambridge: Harvard University Press, 1993.

nthony. "Rhetoric, Region, and Social Science." *Central States Speech Journal* 21.3 (1970) 167–74.

———. "Speech Criticism and American Culture," *Western Journal of Speech Communication* 32.3 (1968) 162–67.

istory." Progressive National Baptist Convention, Inc. Online: http://www.pnbc.org/2oUs/history.htm.

IDS Statistics by Race." *AVERTing HIV and AIDS*. 2008. Online: http://www.avert.org/usastatr.htm.

obgood, Mary Elizabeth. *Dismantling Privilege: An Ethics of Accountability*. Cleveland: Pilgrim, 2000.

odgson, Peter C., and Robert H. King, editors. *Christian Theology: An Introduction to Its Traditions and Tasks*. Minneapolis: Fortress, 1994.

ogan, Patrick Colm. *The Culture of Conformism: Understanding Social Consent*. Durham, : Duke University Press, 2001.

ow Minority Youth Are Being Left Behind by the Graduation Rate Crisis." Urban Institute, February 25, 2004. Online: http://www.urban.org/publications/410936.

eginald. *Race and Manifest Destiny: The Origins of American Racial Anglo-Saxonism*. Cambridge: Harvard University Press, 1981.

unter, Jeannine. "Bishop Eddie Long Returns to the Pulpit." *Huffington Post*, February 1, nline: http://www.huffingtonpost.com/2012/02/01/bishop-eddie-long-crow ned-king_n_1248346.html.

ong. *Clergy Women and Their Worldview: Calling for a New Age*. New York: Praeger, 1987.

*Clergy Worldviews: Now the Men's Voices*. Westport: Praeger, 1995.

Jakes, Thomas Dexter (T. D.). "10 Commandments of Working in a Hostile Environment Series." 2-part CD Series. Dallas: T. D. Jakes Ministries, 2005.

———. "The Battle." *Divine Strategies Series*. Dallas: T. D. Jakes Ministries, 2008.

———. "Chosen." In *T. D. Jakes Classics, Vol. 1*. Dallas: T. D. Jakes Ministries, n.d.

———. "Defeating the Giant of Debt." *Reposition Yourself Series*. Dallas: T. D. Jakes Ministries, 2008.

———. "The Frustration of Liberation," *Liberation Series*. Dallas: T. D. Jakes Ministries, 2006.

———. "Get in the Birth Position," *T.D. Jakes Classics, Vol. 1*. Dallas: T. D. Jakes Ministries, n.d..

———. "The Leading Lady." *God's Leading Ladies Conference [audiotape]* House, 2002.

———. "Repositioning: The Message," *Reposition Yourself Series*. Dallas: T. D. Jakes Ministries, 2008.

Jaudon, Buddy, and Gail Bray, "The Lyons Chronology." *The Tampa Tribune*, 1998. Online: http://www.rickross.com/reference/lyons/lyons27.html.

Jung, Carl G. "On the Psychology of the Unconscious." In *Two Essays on Analytical Psychology*, translated by R. F. C. Hull. Princeton: Princeton University Press, 1966.

King, Martin Luther, Jr. "Where Do We Go from Here: Chaos or Community?" In *Testament of Hope: The Essential Writings and Speeches of Martin Luther King, Jr*, edited by James M. Washington. New York: HarperCollins, 1986.

LaRue, Cleophus James. *The Heart of Black Preaching*. Louisville: Westminster John Press, 2000.

———, editor. *Power in the Pulpit*. Louisville: Westminster John Knox Press, 2002.

Leaver, Robin A., and Joyce Ann Zimmerman, editors. *Liturgy and Music: Lifetime Learning*. Collegeville: Liturgical, 1999.

Lebacqz, Karen, and Joseph D. Driskill. *Ethics and Spiritual Care: A Guide for Pastors, Chaplains and Spiritual Directors*. Nashville: Abingdon, 2000.

———, and Ronald G. Barton, *Sex in the Parish*. Louisville: Westminster John 1991.

Lee, Shayne. *T. D. Jakes: America's New Preacher*. New York: New York 2005.

Lincoln, C. Eric, and Lawrence H. Mamiya. *The Black Church in the African American Experience*. Durham: Duke University Press, 1990.

Long, Eddie L. "2006, the Year of the Man" (2006). Since lawsuits for sexual misconduct were filed against Long in 2010, all of Bishop Long's sermons cited here have become unavailable. Previous sources included Streaming Faith (http://stores.streamingfaith.com/) and New Birth Missionary Baptist Church (http://www.newbirth.org/audio_video_on_demand/). The author retains the recorded sermons purchased through these previous sources in her archives.

———. "The Blood of Jesus and Its Power" (2007).

———. "Conquer and Subdue" (2004).

———. *It's Time to Reclaim Your Territory for the Kingdom*. New Kensington: Whitaker House, 2004.

———. "Our Dominion" (2004).

———. "The Power of Your Testimony" (2007).

———. "Reigning in True Authority: Reigning and Not Maintaining" (2007).

———. "Taking Authority of God's Word" (2006).

ntitled Sermon, September 26, 2010, Praise Cleveland.com, http://www.youtube.com/watch?v=EsVsDOyA4SM.

tto. *Religion and Social Conflict*. Maryknoll, NY: Orbis, 1982.

Marable, Manning. "The Ambiguous Politics of the Black Church." In *How Capitalism Underdeveloped Black America*, 195–214. Cambridge: South End, 1983, 2000.

arl, and Frederick Engels. *The German Ideology Part One, with Selections from Parts Two and Three, Together with Marx's Introduction to a Critique of Political* . New York: International Publishers, 2001.

enzie, Vashti Murphy. "Don't Let Your Wounds Get in the Way," Sermon given at nited Church of Christ, 2008.

———. "Favor Makes a Difference." Sermon preached at Chautauqua Institution, 2009

———. "Fork in the Road Decisions." Sermon preached at Chautauqua Institution, 2009.

———. "From Mess to Miracle: Hold on Hagar." Sermon co-preached with JoAnne ightner-Fuller, Ebenezer A.M.E. Church Women's Conference, 1999.

et's Build Bridges Together." Sermon preached at Bethel A.M.E, Boston, 2012.

———. "People Pleasers." Sermon preached at God is a Wonder Conference, Ebenezer . Church, 2010.

———. "Seven Steps: One Step at a Time," 40th Annual Maryland Black Caucus Celebration, 2010.

———. "The Way In." Sermon preached at Chautauqua Institution, Faith under Fire series, 2003.

McCoy, Charles S. "The Postcritical and Fiduciary Dimension in Polyani and Tillich." *Tradition and Discovery* 22.1 (1995–96) 5–10.

McMickle, Marvin A. *An Encyclopedia of African American Christian Heritage*. Valley Forge: Judson Press, 2002.

*Where Have All the Prophets Gone?: Reclaiming Prophetic Preaching in America*. Cleveland: Pilgrim, 2006.

McWhorter, John H. "Double Consciousness in Black America." *CATO Policy Report* 25.2 April 2003).

Miller, Donald E. "Postdenominational Christianity in the Twenty-First Century." *The ANNALS of the American Academy of Political and Social Science* 558:1 (July 1998)

enry H. *Black Preaching*. New York: Lippincott, 1970.

Mitchem, Stephanie Y. *Name It and Claim It: Prosperity Preaching in the Black Church*. Cleveland: Pilgrim, 2007.

Ravelle. "Bishop Eddie Long Back at New Birth Pulpit?" *The Christian Post*, 6, 2012. Online: http://www.christianpost.com/news/bishop-eddie-long-back-at-new-birth-pulpit-66519.

Musser, Donald W., and Joseph L. Price, editors, *A New Handbook of Christian Theology*. Nashville: Abingdon, 1992.

New Birth Missionary Baptist Church. Online: http://www.newbirth.org/broadcast_schedule.asp.

Kareem. "How the Recession Has Hit Blacks and Latinos," April 16, 2012. nline: http://racerelations.about.com/b/2012/04/16/how-the-recession-has-hit-blacks-and-latinos.htm=.

*Oliver L. Brown et. al. v. the Board of Education of Topeka (KS) et.al.* Brown Foundation. nline: http://brownvboard.org/content/background-overview-summary.

*The Social Teaching of the Black Churches*. Philadelphia: Fortress, 1985.

Poole, Sheila M., and Christian Boone, "Eddie Long Case Officially Dismissed." *Atlanta Journal-Constitution*, May 27, 2011. Online: http://www.ajc.com/news/ dekalb/eddie-long-case-officially-958537.html.

"Prison Statistics." *Bureau of Justice Statistics*, U.S. Department of Justice, September 2008. Online: http://www.ojp.usdoj.gov/bjs/.

Raboteau, Albert J. *Slave Religion: The "Invisible Institution" in the Antebellum South.* York: Oxford University Press, 1978.

Renzetti Claire M., and Raymond M. Lee, editors. *Researching Sensitive Topics* Park, CA: Sage, 1993.

Rey, Terry. "Marketing the Goods of Salvation: Bourdieu on Religion." 34 (2004) 331–43.

Riggs, Marcia. *Plenty Good Room: Women versus Male Power in the Black Church.* Cleveland: Pilgrim, 2003.

Saliers, Don E. *Worship as Theology* Nashville: Abingdon, 1994.

Sanders, Cheryl J. *Empowerment Ethics for a Liberated People: A Path to African American Social Transformation.* Minneapolis: Fortress, 1995.

Slee, Michelle. *The Church in Antioch in the First Century CE: Communion and Conflict.* London: Sheffield Academic, 2003.

Smith, Dorothy E. *The Conceptual Practices of Power: A Feminist Sociology of Knowledge* Boston: Northeastern University Press, 1990.

———. *Writing the Social: Critique, Theory, and Investigations.* Toronto: Toronto Press, 1999.

"Social Action Committee Press Release." *African Methodist Episcopal Church* 2008. Online: http://www.streetprophets.com/storyonly/2008/3/24/13404/5738.

Steven, Alexis. "Bishop Eddie Long Accused in Investment Scam." *The Atlanta Journal-Constitution*, October 19, 2011. Online: http://www.ajc.com/news/bishop-eddie-long-accused-1206060.html 05/01/12.

Swartz, David. "Bridging the Study between Culture and Religion: Pierre Bourdieu's Political Economy of Symbolic Power." *Sociology of Religion* 57.1 (1996)

———. *Culture and Power: The Sociology of Pierre Bourdieu.* Chicago: Chicago Press, 1997.

Taylor, Gardner C. *Essential Taylor.* Audiotape. Valley Forge, PA: Judson, 2000.

———. *Words of Gardner Taylor: 50 Years of Timeless Treasures.* Valley Forge, P 2002.

———. *The Words of Gardner Taylor: NBC Radio Sermons 1959–1970* Edward L. Taylor. Valley Forge, PA: Judson, 1999.

Taylor, Mark Lewis. *Remembering Esperanza: A Cultural-Political Theology for North American Praxis.* Minneapolis: Fortress, 2004.

"The American Community—Blacks: 2004." *American Community Survey Reports* Census Bureau (February 2007).

"The Justice System." *Nation Black United Fund*, September 27, 2008. O nbuf.org/statistics.

"The Lyons' Trial: The Aftermath." *St. Petersburg Times*, 2006. Online: http://www.sptimes. com/News2/lyons/default.html.

Trimiew, Darryl M. *God Bless the Child That's Got Its Own: The Economic Rights Debate.* Atlanta: Scholars, 1997.

Wartenburg, Thomas. *The Forms of Power: An Essay in Social Ontology* Temple University Press, 1989.

On Charisma and Institution Building. Ed. and intro. S.N. Eisenstadt. Chicago: University of Chicago Press, 1968.

From Max Weber: Essays in Sociology, H.H. Gerth and C Wright Mills (eds.). New xford University Press, 1958.

The Theory of Social and Economic Organization. Edited by Talcott Parsons and enderson. New York: The Free Press, 1947.

"Welcome to Transformation Church." Transformation Church, August 28, 2008. Online: http://www.transformationchurch.org/believe.php.

West, Traci C. Disruptive Christian Ethics. Louisville: Westminster John Knox, 2006.

Space for Faith, Sexual Desire, and Ethical Black Ministerial Practices." In Loving the Body, edited by Anthony B. Pinn and Dwight N. Hopkins. New York: Palgrave McMillan, 2004.

Williams, Delores S. Sisters in the Wilderness: The Challenge of Womanist God-Talk Maryknoll: Orbis, 1996.

eith E. The Epistemology of Religious Experience. New York: Cambridge niversity, 1993

Young, Iris Marion. Justice and the Politics of Difference. Princeton: Princeton University Press, 1990.

Zimmerman, Joyce Ann. Liturgy and Hermeneutics. Collegeville, MD: Liturgical, 1999.